P7-CHD-565

WHAT EVERY CHRISTIAN SHOULD KNOW ABOUT

MONEY MANAGEMENT

MONTY McKINNON
Foreword by David Mainse

100 HUNTLEY STREET

SPECIAL EDITION

 A ministry of
Crossroads Christian Communications Inc.

In Canada:

Crossroads Christian
Communications Inc.
100 Huntley Street
Toronto, Ontario
M4Y 2L1

Bus: (416) 961-8001

In the USA:

Crossroads Christian
Communications Inc.
Box 486
Niagara Falls, NY
14302

Prayer: (416) 961-1500

MASTER FINANCIAL PLANNING SERVICES INC.,
P.O. Box 131, Newmarket, Ontario, L3Y 4W3

What Every Christian Should Know About
Money Management

Copyright 1988 by Master Financial Planning Services Inc.

1st Printing – 1989

Printed in Canada by Harmony Printing Limited

Cover copy and concept by Univision Marketing Group Ltd.

ISBN 0-9693761-0-3

All rights reserved. No part of this publication may be reproduced, stored in a retrieval system, or transmitted in any form or presented as a seminar or educational material by any means electronic, mechanical, photocopy, slide, recording or otherwise, without prior permission of the copyright owner, except for brief quotation in critical reviews or articles.

Unless otherwise stated scripture quoted is:

Scripture taken from the New American Standard Bible,
1960, 1962, 1963, 1968, 1971, 1972, 1973, 1975,
1977 The Lockman Foundation. Used by permission.

Other Sources:

Scripture quotations are from the Amplified New Testament, 1954, 1958, 1987 by The Lockman Foundation. Used by permission.

"From the Holy Bible: New International Version.
Copyright 1973, 1978, 1984 International Bible Society. Used by permission of Zondervan Bible Publishers."

An effort has been made to acknowledge all sources used in this material. If inadvertently any source has been omitted, please advise our organization and any error will be corrected in future publications.

DEDICATION

I am extremely grateful to the Lord for His exceptional favour given to this organization. In particular, that He would allow us the privilege to present this material, pertaining to His principles of money management.

ACKNOWLEDGEMENTS

I would like to acknowledge the support and help given to me by my associates, friends and especially my wife, Donna. Her constant encouragement has always provided support when it was needed the most.

In particular, I offer my sincere thanks and gratitude to the following: Dr. Brian Davis, Mr. William Wagner, Mr. Barry Matthews, Dr. Harry Heinrichs, Mr. James Rankin, Mr. Walter Matte, Mrs. Susan Walton, Mr. Erwin Van Laar and Mr. John Dell.

Also special thanks to Dr. Brian Davis for his editorial assistance.

SPECIAL ACKNOWLEDGEMENT

I would like to thank the following ministries for their support and their spirit of co-operation in helping with the distribution of this book: 100 Huntley Street, World Vision Canada and The Peoples Church, Toronto.

Preface

Many people, Christians and non-Christians, have difficulty in managing their finances. Sometimes our difficulties stem from an apparent inability to "make ends meet"; we have a negative cash flow, as the saying goes. Perhaps our financial circumstances have suddenly changed and we cannot seem to adjust our family budget to the change. We are not sure how to go about it—where to start, who to consult. Sometimes, we feel that we can't share our concerns with family or others because we are not sure where to start or because we feel that we ought to be able "to go it alone".

Consequently, nothing gets done and our difficulties worsen. On the other hand, we may not be experiencing immediate financial difficulties. Nevertheless, we are aware of the future and what it brings with it – retirement and eventual disposal of our estate. We have some healthy concerns about providing for our retirement years but perhaps do not really know how best to go about it.

We are aware, of course, that eventually our estate will have to be wound up in our absence and we feel some concern for those we leave behind. We want our estate and monies to be put to their best use for our spouse, our children, and, for many of us, our church. Even so, it is not a pleasant topic to contemplate, so we "put it off till another day". We procrastinate and, suddenly, it is too late, for we are no longer in a position to control the circumstances and exercise our wishes.

The purpose of this material is to enable you to take control of your financial situation now, to exercise that control in planning for the future, and to maintain control of how your estate and monies are used after you have gone. This material on financial planning will enable Christians and non-Christians alike to feel a sense of security that comes from efficient management of day-to-day resources and adequate preparation for the future for ourselves and our loved ones.

I hope that this information will enable you to take steps to live a life that is pleasing to God—and in turn enabling you to be a blessing to others.

Monty McKinnon, B.B.M.

Foreword

Monty McKinnon has provided a much needed service to Canadians. There are several books in the market on "money management" from a Christian perspective that are written by Americans. I'm happy for the Americans because it addresses their tax laws, their investment laws, etc. However, those books have not met the needs of Canadians. Now, advice which financial managers would charge large sums to provide concerning specific Canadian concerns, laws, etc., are presented to us in this book. Of course, that's only a small part of Monty's research.

This book is grounded firmly on God's Word and, while the Bible does not profess to be a financial management textbook, it does contain eternal principles which, when followed, provide a basis for wise money management. The foundation of these principles is in God's righteousness and justice.

Monty McKinnon is highly qualified academically and experientially. The practical counsel between these covers is not sent down from an ivory tower as some kind of an untried theory, but it has been proven again and again to work!

When I was a college student, a guest lecturer encouraged us to establish an adequate filing system based on his filing system. He called the system "B.F.U." He said the only way to be successful with this filing system was illustrated by those letters. They stood for:

B – "Begin at once."
F – "Follow instructions."
U – "Use it constantly."

I've never forgotten that, and I used his filing system for a number of years until I had a secretary who took over. I can guarantee that if you will begin at once, follow instructions and use it constantly, Monty McKinnon's *What Every Christian Should Know About Money Management* will work for you so that you will be blessed and, in turn, you will be able to bless others more than ever.

In Christ's Love and Service,
David Mainse, Host of "100 Huntley Street"

Table of Contents

Chapter Four
Personal Planning Stragegies

Chapter Five
The Importance of Estate Planning

Chapter Six
Tax Planning Strategies

Chapter Seven
Planning For Retirement

Chapter Eight
Handling Financial Freedom

How to Use this Material

The eight Chapters contained in this book represent both information and instruction about specific financial topics in everyone's life and a sequential learning plan which Donna and I practice in our own lives. The reader may study and apply the information contained in any given chapter to his or her life or may choose to work through the book chapter by chapter, in order to obtain a fuller understanding of the relationship of the different topics.

The statistical and factual information contained in the book is obtained from reputable sources, including the governments of the Provinces of Canada. As such, this material is to be considered accurate at the time of publication and Master Financial Planning Services Inc. cannot accept responsibility for subsequent changes in information concerning these sources. Master Financial Planning Services Inc. and it's representatives are not engaged in rendering legal, accounting, investment advisory or other professional service.The advice and recommendations contained here are based upon our analysis of the situation as it presently exists. While most of these concepts are unlikely to be affected by financial events in the near future, some changes, for example, in tax reform, or other areas may require the reader to obtain updated recommendations from his/her financial adviser.

The information provided herewith, whether composed of computer software illustrations, analyses, reports, hand written/drawn illustrations, brochures, prototype/specimen documentation etc., are entirely for educational purposes.

While great care has been taken to ensure the accuracy of the statements and information contained in our publication, no liability is assumed for financial or legal decisions based upon them.

Chapter One

So, Who Owns It Anyway?

YOUR GOALS

At the close of this chapter, you should be able to:

a) explain the principle of good stewardship,

b) explain why financial planning is necessary,

c) identify several barriers to successful money management,

d) examine your financial needs and behaviours with a view to deciding to take action; and

e) compare world and biblical principles related to money management.

A. FIRST PRINCIPLES

In almost every book I have read on the concept of stewardship, the author begins with a discussion on the subject of the ownership of our possessions. Ownership is an area that seems to present some Christians with difficulty. I was surprised to learn that many are not thrilled with the idea that someone else is responsible for their success and actually owns all the "things" they possess. Yet, the simple truth is that someday, someone else will own all the things we call "ours"! That is a sobering thought.

Certainly, no one objects to ownership, providing that this ownership is of some use to that individual. For example, most of us are delighted with the thought that the Lord has placed His seal of ownership on us.[1] Have you ever noticed how many so-called non-Christians will call on the Lord in their day of trouble. Yet, most of us tend to give only a passing thought to the concept of the Lord as the truly rightful owner of all of our possessions, as the following verses tell us.

The earth is the Lord's and everything in it, the world, and all who live in it. (Ps.24:1)

The heavens are yours, and yours also the earth; you founded the world and all that is in it. (Ps.89:11)

The silver is mine and the gold is mine, declares the Lord Almighty. (Hag.2:8)

If we examine some of the early Hebrew history as it pertains to ownership we can not escape the fact that the Lord is the rightful owner of all we possess. When the families of Israel went into the promised land, they divided the land by lot. The promised land was given to them by God. They didn't earn it, they didn't buy it, it was given to them as a gift from God.[2] In the book of Proverbs we read:

The lot is cast into the lap, but its every decision is from the Lord. (Pr. 16:33)

Therefore, we have a lot because it was God who gave it to us. Even today, we still use the same terminology. If we were to examine the legal description of our home, we would find that it is registered as Lot 25 or some similar number. Even when we purchase a new home, the builder will show us a site plan and request that we select a Lot.

As Christians, we have a large responsibility, by virtue of the "Trust" the Lord has placed at our disposal, to exercise wisdom in all of our financial and business dealings. We must exercise the best of care over the assets which the Lord has placed at our disposal and, to the best of our ability, cause those assets to grow for Him.

This is the principle of good stewardship. Stewardship is not a question of ownership as much as it is a recognition of "loanership".

Christian stewardship is a demonstration of our **"faithfulness"**. If we prove ourselves in some of the simple tasks that the Lord has for us, then He will put us in charge of more and, likely, greater things. Then, we will hear Him say:

Well done, good and faithful servant! You have been faithful with a few things; I will put you in charge of many things. Come and share your master's happiness! (Mt.25:23)

When the Master returns, we will be called forth to be accountable for what we have done with His investment. Did we exercise wisdom? Did we squander and waste his resources on foolishness? Have we used His possessions to lay up treasures in heaven?[3] Did we feed the hungry and clothe the naked?[4]

Financial Planning is necessary, if we are to achieve our financial goals and practice good stewardship. The intention in planning is to get us from where we stand today, financially, to where we wish to stand at some predetermined point in the future.

Christian Financial Planning is wise stewardship. At its base is the acknowledgement that God is the rightful owner of all that we possess. The Apostle Paul, in his letter to Timothy, told him to do the following:

> Command those who are rich in this present world not to be arrogant nor to put their hope in wealth, which is so uncertain, but to put their hope in God, who richly provides us with everything for our enjoyment. Command them to do good, to be rich in good deeds, and to be generous and willing to share. In this way they will lay up treasure for themselves as a firm foundation for the coming age, so that they may take hold of the life that is truly life. (1 Ti.6:17-19)

If we, as Christians, are to "take hold of the life that is truly life", it becomes important for us to carefully assess the work that God is doing and to support that work of the Lord as He directs. We are to be generous and to be rich with "good deeds". We are not to squander His resources, but, rather, to invest His resources with wisdom. This is "the life that is truly life".

Success in the financial areas of our life is dependent on our need to establish **correct priorities,** especially if we expect to receive any blessing from the Lord. That is why He reminds us to seek His kingdom and righteousness first, after which all our other needs will be met.[5]

I suspect that if we were to remember only those two points, that is, to seek His kingdom and to seek His righteousness, then many of us would be much better off. Many of us will be familiar with the problems arising from time commitment to our job. It can result in us seeing very little of our spouse, not having time to play with our children, and not having time to go to church because we have to work on Sunday at home or at the office. When we earnestly commit our life to the Lord, He will provide us with the time for these other activities.

When we are in debt, the road to financial freedom appears long and difficult. My experience has shown me that many do not even bother to try to break free of their debt because they feel hopelessly lost.

There is an answer.

The solution rests with a commitment ..... to the Lord Jesus Christ.

He tells us to give Him our problems because He can handle all of them. He does not become tired and weary but rather He tells us to learn from Him and He will give us rest.

> *Come to me, all you who are weary and burdened, and I will give you rest. Take my yoke upon you and learn from me, for I am gentle and humble in heart, and you will find rest for your souls. For my yoke is easy and my burden is light. (Mt. 11:28-30)*

It is also important to remember that we are to give Him all of our problems. This includes our finances as well as other areas which would distract us from giving all of our attention to Him. You are encouraged to cast all your anxiety on him because he cares for you.[6]

The key is for us to remain faithful to the end of the race. Have you ever noticed how often we become discouraged because of our particular financial difficulty? We try to save some money for a rainy day but it always seems to be raining. The insurance premium comes calling at our door or there is an unexpected long distance call or the family auto needs servicing or the children are going on a special "field trip" at school, and there goes our savings. It is easy to become discouraged and to want to throw in the towel and give up.

Discouragement is a weapon frequently used against us. It is discouragement that causes many Christians to give up and fail to attain the abundant life promised all Christians in John's Gospel.[7] However, despite our circumstances, real or imagined, we may look to the Lord for direction and help in times of difficulty. We can follow David's example when he said, "I sought the Lord, and he answered me; he delivered me from all my fears".[8]

To "seek the Lord" implies that we will not always find Him in our first outing or as soon as we start searching for Him. Rather, we must keep on seeking Him and keep on persevering in our efforts to find Him. The promise which is given to those who diligently seek Him is that He will answer us, as He did King David.

Most of us become discouraged about our finances because we know how easy it was to get into debt, yet how difficult it is to get out of debt. It will mean for many of us that the dreams and desires which we have for our family must be put on the shelf for a while. This reality makes us sad and frustrated as we desire to provide for our family.

Sometimes, we are tempted to use non-Christian means to become successful. I frequently receive telephone calls asking me to evaluate some new idea or new product that needs immediate investment. There is a "guaranteed" high rate of return promised if the potential investor would act today.

My father taught me not to rush into things and to certainly investigate before I invest. This is sound advice and it has kept me from making painful mistakes. The problem with this type of get-rich-quick solution is that it is a band-aid approach and the heart of the problem is still there. Besides, my experience has taught me that the get-rich-quick method seldom ever works. This is another temptation that we struggle to avoid in our lives.

Yet, it is difficult to watch others who cheat on their taxes, or steal from their place of employment, or perhaps show all the signs of prosperity gained from shady business dealings. They seem to be successful, while we struggle to make ends meet. Many want to taste this level of success. The question must be: are we willing to pay such a high price for a success which is only temporary and will soon disappear? Paul, in his letter to the Romans, tells us that the wages of sin is death, but the gift of God is eternal life in Christ Jesus.[9]

The gift of eternal life is too precious to be compromised. We cannot afford to be involved in practices that endanger our integrity and credibility. We are instructed:

Do not fret because of evil men or be envious of those who do wrong; for like the grass they will soon wither, like green plants they will soon die away. Trust in the Lord and do good; dwell in the land and enjoy safe pasture. Delight yourself in the Lord and he will give you the desires of your heart. (Ps.37:1-4)

As we ponder over the above statement, it confirms in our heart that it is a waste of time to fret over the temporary success of some "evil doer" when we could be delighting ourselves in the Lord who will supply all of our needs according to His riches in glory in Christ Jesus.[10] Not only is He the rightful owner of everything we manage but He cares for us in such detail that even the very hairs of our head are all numbered.[11]

He will be our constant source of protection and has promised to rebuke the devourer for us, so that he may not destroy the fruits of the ground.[12] In addition, He has promised to be our source of strength in times of weakness:

> *I will strengthen you and help you; I will uphold you with my righteous right hand. (Isa.41:10)*

The Lord has always been faithful. We don't find a promise that He doesn't fulfil, for God is not a man that He should lie, nor a son of man, that He should change His mind.[13]

As we begin this adventure in financial planning, let me suggest that you consider examining your willingness to commit your financial needs and behaviour to the Lord, for we are told to trust in the Lord with all our heart and lean not on our own understanding. We are encouraged to acknowledge Him, and He will make our paths straight.[14]

As the information in this book begins to unfold, we will see some of the solutions the Lord has provided for us in the area of financial planning.

If finances have never been one of your strengths, don't worry, this book will explain in detail everything you need to know to get you started on the road to financial freedom and independence. (remember that a glossary of financial terms has been included at the back of this book in case there are terms you are not familiar with.) Every journey starts with a first step. Will you take your first step today? We acknowledge that financial planning is not an easy task for everyone. Perhaps that is why Jesus talked so much about money in the various parables given for our instruction.

B. SUMMARY

Principles In Conflict

WORLD	BIBLICAL
Focus On Self	Focus On God
Operate On Credit	Owe Nothing To Anyone
Keep What You Earn	Give To Others In Need
Trust In Your Own Judgement	Trust In The Lord For Guidance
What I Make Is Mine	The Lord Is The Rightful Owner Of All
Get It At Any Cost	The Wages Of Sin Is Death
Do It Your Way	Jesus Is The Way
Wealth And Honour Among Men Counts	Eternal Life And Honour Before God Counts Most
Integrity And Credibility Are Expendable	Righteousness Before God Is Essential

Have you considered...

1. What is the principle of good stewardship? Explain it in your own words.

2. How you are applying good stewardship in your money management? What are the barriers that are preventing you from applying good stewardship in your money management?

3. Examining your present money management practices with a view to improving them? If so, indicate two areas where you feel financial planning may best help you.

4. What changes you may have to make in order to meet your needs. Take a sheet of paper and divide it into two columns. In the left column indicate your financial needs. In the right column indicate the necessary changes.

5. Giving two examples of circumstances where perseverance resulted in obtaining a desired goal.

6. How others have become financially successful based on applying biblical principles in their lives.

7. Finding five different references to the handling of money in both the Old Testament and in the New Testament.

Chapter Two

Plan Now, Save Later

YOUR GOALS

At the close of this chapter, you should be able to:

a) list several reasons why planning is necessary for money management,

b) calculate the approximate value of your estate,

c) identify short and long range goals and objectives that you would like to reach in your financial planning,

d) develop jointly agreed family goals and objectives for managing your finances; and

e) identify the key participants in terms of commitment to managing your finances.

A. INTRODUCTION

1. Money Management – The Possible Dream!

It is a remarkable fact that Jesus spoke more about money management **(financial planning)** than He did about many other important areas such as prayer, faith, and eternal life. Almost half of the parables deal with money matters as their principal topic. God is extremely concerned that Christians handle well the material blessings that He sends their way.[1]

God has said that the wealth of the world is His.[2] He has also said that He will meet all our needs[3] and that if we are Christians, then we are also heirs to the promises of God.[4]

Notwithstanding, Christians cannot afford to act irresponsibly and still expect to receive blessings from God.[5] Fortunately, clear directions are given in the scriptures whereby we may follow God's plan to achieve our desires or goals.[6]

Planning, careful forethought, and the exercise of common sense are considered by the world to be obvious in embarking upon any endeavour, especially in the area of finances. It should not come as a surprise to us to learn that such principles have a sound biblical foundation.[7]

2. Why Plan?

We are taught that it is **wisdom** and **understanding** which form the basis for success in any endeavour and that by application of these resources success may be acquired.[8]

It is unwise not to consider if our resources are sufficient for what we wish to accomplish.[9] Equally, it is unwise to forget that total reliance on our own ideas is not the complete answer.[10]

Planning......

Brings All The Pieces Together

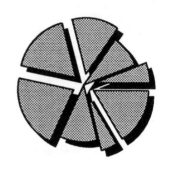

B. MAKING THE PLANNING PROCESS WORK FOR YOU

Step 1. Measuring Your Financial Fitness

Before we start out on our annual vacation, we must first decide where we are going, what hotels will fit into the budget, what meals will be consumed at restaurants, how much money we will spend and what will be left over for personal shopping. Once we have decided that our resources are sufficient for the proposed holiday, away we go.

The same principle in planning applies here. You must first conduct a self evaluation so that you know your current state of affairs. This is what I did when I started on the road to financial freedom. Once you know approximately what your financial picture looks like, you can then make the necessary decisions to achieve your personal and family goals.

Planning is a biblical principle demonstrated throughout the Bible. Can you imagine trying to build an ark, like Noah, or a temple, like Solomon, or leading the Israelites, like Moses, without having first made a plan? The **greatest plan** of all, devised and carefully implemented by God, is, of course, the plan for salvation.

Do you have a written financial plan for you and your family?

Most of us do not have any written or specific plans concerning our finances.

A barrier to preparing a financial plan is the myth that the plan will take many hours to prepare and then will limit your freedom. Just the opposite is true. A plan sets you on course to freedom and does not require much time either to implement or maintain.

It is easy to procrastinate and promise that you will prepare your plan tomorrow. But the Bible has a teaching on that very thought: "Now listen, you who say, 'Today or tomorrow we will go to this or that city, spend a year there, carry on business and make money.' Why, you do not even know what will happen tomorrow."[11] It seems, therefore, that the best thing for us to do is to get started – **Now!**

Case Study:

> Bill and Flo Cash are your typical middle-aged couple. They have two wonderful children, Johnny and Tilly, in their teens, and live in a modest home somewhere in your city. Bill works very hard for his employer and has received two promotions in the past two years. Flo has a position working as a legal secretary. They have many financial problems, but the one that concerns them the most is that they never seem to have enough cash flow! Let's examine their situation in more detail as they develop a financial plan to meet their needs.

On the following pages you will find that they have completed:

1. A Personal Evaluation Questionnaire

2. A Summary Asset Evaluation Form

The questionnaire has a yes/no format and Flo and Bill have completed this together by checking off the answer which best represents their situation at present. It is important for Bill and Flo to indicate their actual situation and not what they have been intending to accomplish. This form is private between Bill and Flo, as your form will be between you and your spouse. You will find a blank form for your use in Appendix A.

Bill and Flo will now complete, as best they can, The Summary Asset Evaluation form which is to be completed together, by estimating figures where necessary. Following the example of Flo and Bill, use the form provided for you in Appendix A. Fill in the blank line opposite each item which applies to your present financial situation. Use approximate numbers rounded to the nearest hundred dollars. Some of the items may be more difficult to determine but try to complete all areas using your best "guesstimate" where necessary. The more accurate you are, the more reliable your financial plan will be as we go through the following steps.

First, total your assets and your liabilities and place these figures in the appropriate space under the heading Net Worth. Second, subtract the liabilities from your assets and place this figure in the space marked Net Estate.

The figure in Net Estate represents the approximate current value of your estate before any deductions for possible taxation have been applied.

PERSONAL EVALUATION QUESTIONNAIRE

	YES	NO
1. Do you have a written financial plan?	☐	☒
2. Have you and your spouse prepared your "Will"?	☐	☒
3. Do you know the amount of your family debt?	☐	☒
4. Do you have money left over at the end of the month?	☐	☒
5. Have you started an R.R.S.P.?	☐	☒
6. Do you have a plan to pay off your mortgage early?	☐	☒
7. Do you have a plan for making future investments?	☐	☒
8. Do you worry about paying bills and meeting financial obligations?	☒	☐
9. Do you pay all of your bills on time?	☐	☒
10. Have you had to borrow money to pay off debts or taxes?	☒	☐
11. Do you hold a second job in order to meet your financial obligations?	☐	☒
12. Are you presently "tithing" your income on a regular basis?	☐	☒
13. Do you have more than one automobile?	☒	☐
14. Do you plan your shopping to avoid impulse buying?	☐	☒
15. Do you discuss major purchases with your spouse before a purchase?	☒	☐
16. Do you always receive a tax receipt for your charitable giving?	☐	☒
17. Do you use personal credit cards?	☒	☐
18. Do you know the balance of your bank accounts?	☐	☒

Source: T. Giordano, CBN, Virginia Beach

Name: __BILL & FLO.__

SUMMARY ASSET EVALUATION FORM

ASSETS		LIABILITIES	
Chequing Accounts	$ 450	Bank Loans	$ 4000
Savings Accounts	500	Charge Accounts	3600
Life Ins. Cash Value		Monthly Bills O/S	700
Money Owed You		Other	
Gold/Silver			
Securities/Stocks		Mortgage/Home	125,000
CSB's	600	Cottage	
Mutual Funds		Other	
GIC's			
Business		Debts/Individuals	1500
Other		Credit Union	
Personal Property		**Loans**	
Automobiles	6,500	Automobiles	2000
House Furnishings	15,000	Rec. Vehicles	
Antiques/Jewelry		Other	
Real Estate			
Home	170,000	**TOTAL LIABILITY**$ 136,800	
Cottage			
Condo			
Other			
Pension		**NET WORTH**	
Company	2500		
RRSP's		Total Assets	$ 195,550
Annuities		Less	
Insurance Face Value		Total Liabilities	$ 136,800
Insurance FV Spouse			
Other		Net Estate	$ 58,750
TOTAL ASSETS	$ 195,550	Dated_____	

Step 2. Getting On Track

a. Define Goals

Most individuals have some vague idea as to what their goals might be. On the other hand, it is highly unlikely that any of these goals are written down anywhere.

The Apostle Paul spoke of having a goal when he said, "I press on toward the goal to win the prize for which God has called me heavenward in Christ Jesus."[12] Perhaps, for you, the prize Paul mentions is attaining financial freedom, or being able to do more for the Lord in some specific area.

Your ideas for better management of your money may involve putting money aside for a special vacation, for investing in an education fund for your children, for reducing expenditures through the use of credit cards, for increasing your tithing and offerings, or for purchasing tax-deferred retirement savings plans. Such ideas are all very fine but, unless they are turned into practical and reachable goals, they may become a burden to us rather than a blessing.

Regardless of your reasons for wanting to make changes in your financial situation, you must establish clear, concrete goals that are sensible in terms of your lifestyle. The situation may change as time goes on and the goals can be amended to reflect the changed circumstances. Setting a goal that is both unrealistic and inflexible is unwise and can become a source of aggravation rather than a positive and helpful experience.

The importance of carefully determining your goals is emphasized in the expression **"I press on"** which indirectly speaks of problems that must be overcome and that your path may not be a short one. Your goal will require you to persevere regardless of all obstacles, big or small. We are told that the man who perseveres under trial will receive the crown of life that God promised to those who love him.[13] It is most important that we continue to persevere.

A written record of your intent to manage your finances is a major step. Initially, you can state your goals in broad terms without pausing to consider their practicality and whether or not they can be met over a short or long period of time. Bill and Flo took a few moments and jotted down some ideas for managing their money in the future. Using a blank

31

sheet, jot down your ideas for managing your money from now on. Once you have done this, look carefully at what you have written and adjust the statements until they are clear. Then decide which of these goal statements you want to achieve in one year. These are your short term goals.

Our goals need to be measurable, realistic and achievable. By a measurable goal, we are referring to, say, saving one hundred dollars. Your progress is easily measured, as opposed to, say, walking closer with the Lord. The later is worth while but difficult to measure. When I have been speaking at various churches or other meetings, I have met many individuals who told me that they have goals. They told me that if they had more money they could do more for charity or pay off outstanding debts or give some money to relatives. It all sounds good, but, in reality, they are telling me their dreams, not specific goals.

I remember when I purchased my first new home. I had given the builder a $400 deposit, then selected a lot and house plan. It was then that I realized that I now had a specific goal. I would visit the house site on weekends and watch the progress with great excitement and anticipation, until that final closing day when I could move into my new home. Having a specific goal kept me on track.

b. Immediate Needs

Short Term Goals are those goals which you plan to accomplish in a one year period. Just like Bill and Flo, review your list, then:

1) Select three goals you would want to accomplish this year.

2) Prioritize your three goals (put a (1) against the most important).

3) Can your goals be measured? Are they realistic and achievable?

4) Bill and Flo made a written record of their three goals. Using the forms provided in Appendix A, record your goals and compare them with those written by your spouse. Now, from the possible list of six goals, jointly prioritize your most important three.

c. In The Long Run

Term Goals are those goals which you plan to accomplish in a period of time longer than one year. Again, Flo and Bill made a written record of their long term goals. We need to do the same.

1) From your list, choose up to three goals you would want to accomplish in a period which would take more than one year.

2) Prioritize your three goals as you did for your short term goals.

3) Can your goals be measured? Are they realistic and achievable?

4) Bill and Flo also recorded their three long term goals. As before, we will compare our goals with those written by our spouse and from the possible list of six goals, decide on your most important three.

Name: **BILL & FLO.**

SHORT TERM GOALS

Prioritized Goals BILL

1. VACATION
2. REPLACE CAR
3. MAKE INVESTMENT

Prioritized Goals FLO.

1. PAY BILLS
2. INCREASE CASH FLOW
3. SEND CHILDREN TO PRIVATE SCHOOL

COMBINED SHORT TERM GOALS

1. INCREASE CASH FLOW
2. BEGIN REGULAR SAVINGS PROGRAM
3. CHILDREN'S EDUCATION

Name: __BILL & FLO.__

LONG TERM GOALS

Prioritized Goals BILL

1. COTTAGE
2. RETIREMENT
3. GET OUT OF DEBT

Prioritized Goals FLO.

1. GET OUT OF DEBT
2. MONEY FOR CHILDREN'S EDUCATION
3. RETIREMENT

COMBINED LONG TERM GOALS

1. GET OUT OF DEBT
2. RETIREMENT SAVINGS PROGRAM
3. UNIVERSITY EDUCATION

Step 3. Getting From Here To There

Bill and Flo now have a clear understanding of what they both want to accomplish. They are heading in the same direction. Often, when I have been counselling with couples, I frequently find that the husband's efforts and goals and the wife's efforts are headed in opposite directions.

Once they come to a point of understanding what each other is trying to accomplish, then real progress can be made. This is what we will find with Flo and Bill as they move together instead of apart. Bill's prioritized goals are not the same as Flo's. Bill is more interested in acquiring material things, whereas Flo is more interested in saving money and getting out of debt.

Objectives and Goals are not the same. Objectives are those methods that will be used to reach our goals. Suppose that Bill and Flo have agreed that their number one goal is to be free from debt in a period of two years. Some of the objectives we might expect them to accomplish in order to reach their goal would be as follows:

- Stop ALL credit spending

- Use cash or cheque for all purchases
- Use coupons when food shopping
- Shop only from a list
- Begin tithing their incomes
- Have the same person do all the shopping
- Discuss and agree on all purchases over fifty dollars
- Begin a regular savings program
- Prepare a family budget
- Seek professional counselling
- Adopt a weekly allowance for each other
- Begin reading articles relating to financial planning

a. Short Term Objectives For Short Term Goals

Objectives, for short term goals should be those activities which will enable us to accomplish our goals in less than one year.

Bill and Flo were careful to avoid the tendency to create or define a large number of goals or objectives. For them, too many goals and objectives would lead to discouragement and frustration. If this were allowed to happen, then they might have wanted to quit trying to achieve their goals. We must be careful that we do not become discouraged, frustrated and quit because we have too many goals and objectives.

Remember that the Apostle Paul warned of this when he stated:

> No temptation has seized you except what is common to man. And God is faithful; he will not let you be tempted beyond what you can bear. But when you are tempted, he will also provide a way out so that you can stand up under it. (1Co.10:13)

Examine your first goal, the one you gave highest priority to during the one-year period. Jot down on paper, what objectives you believe you can employ which will enable you to meet your major goal. For example, Flo and Bill decided that they would adopt a weekly allowance for personal spending.

Review your list for clarity and then set your priorities, putting the objective you feel will accomplish the most, as number one, on the forms provided at the back of this book. You and your spouse can then discuss these objectives from the point of view of practicality and commitment.

Finally, use the lower half of the same form to record your jointly decided, and prioritized objectives for the goal. These agreed or combined objectives may be recorded for each of the three short term goals using the pages in the Appendix. These sheets become a permanent record of your decision to manage your finances over a one-year period.

ESTABLISHING OBJECTIVES
For Goal # 1 SHORT TERM

Bill's Prioritized Objectives   **Flo's Prioritized Objectives**

1. PREPARE BUDGET   1. DESTROY CREDIT CARDS

2. WEEKLY ALLOWANCE   2. STOP EATING OUT

3. STOP CREDIT CARD SPENDING   3. COMPARISON SHOPPING

COMBINED OBJECTIVES

1. ESTABLISH FAMILY BUDGET

2. WEEKLY ALLOWANCE

3. DESTROY CREDIT CARDS

b. Long Term Objectives For Long Term Goals

This section is more challenging than objectives for short term goals. We are speaking of those objectives which take longer than a year to accomplish in order to reach a long term goal. For example, our long term goal may be to complete a certificate program in biblical studies. However, this program will require twelve different courses over a period of three years. Our objectives, therefore, may be to complete four courses in the first year and five courses in the second and the remainder the last year. Your goal may be to pay off your $20,000 remaining mortgage during the next four years. If your objective was to make a lump sum payment each year-end of $5,000, your goal is reached in four years.

Complete the forms in Appendix A for your long term goals as you did for the short term goals.

Step 4. Financial Freedom Requires Commitment

True commitment to your financial planning goals and objectives is essential. It is important to realize that you are not alone in this commitment.

First, you should be aware that it is God's will that we should be successful. The Bible contains much evidence that He wants to bless us with all good things.[14]

Secondly, our commitment is strengthened if it is a shared one. This means agreement within our family. Further, we are told that, where two of us are in agreement over a matter, God will hear us and meet our needs.[15] However, it is extremely important to recognize two things. Our agreement is not on its own sufficient to produce the desired results and certainly not necessarily immediately (recall the sowing and reaping principle).[16]

The Lord's commitment to your plan is essential; it must be in agreement with His desire for your life. We must know what we want and we must make our needs known to the Lord.[17] In order to accomplish this, we must be in right standing with God.[18]

C. SUMMARY

1. The wealth of the world is God's.

2. God's will is for His people to be successful.

3. God is concerned that we practice good financial management of His resources.

4. We are to seek wisdom, understanding and good counsel, as we manage our affairs.

5. Our decisions should be agreed upon by our immediate family.

6. We should commit our plans to the Lord for His approval and direction.

Questions For Review

1. State several reasons why God would be concerned that we practice good financial management.
2. Give several reasons why it is important for a Christian to seek counsel on financial matters.
3. Indicate some benefits you would receive from establishing both long and short range goals.
4. Explain what shared commitment does for planning.

Chapter Three

Debt-Conflicting Values

YOUR GOALS

At the close of this chapter, you should be able to:

a) compare and contrast the traditional and Christian approaches to financial planning,

b) identify God's requirements of the Christian in financial matters,

c) list at least ten steps to obtaining financial freedom,

d) examine your lifestyle to determine the influence of the world on your financial behaviour; and

e) make decisions that will enable you to become debt free.

A. INTRODUCTION

In a time of conflicting values, it is important to understand the principles of money management. This chapter will enable us to focus our thinking on His way of handling our finances.

B. THE WORLD'S PLAN AND GOD'S PLAN

We are encouraged daily, through advertising, to acquire material possessions and to attempt to accumulate wealth. Frequently, the methods used emphasize the get-rich-quick approach or deferred-payment principle. It is suggested to us that we need some product now and that without this product our life and lives of our family members can never be complete.

In today's world, it is important, we are told, to establish a good "credit rating". There was a time when this was a measure of an individual's stability and reliability. It indicated that our financial resources were adequate and that we managed our funds well.

Today, credit tends to be self-serving, providing a means of obtaining new things that we might otherwise have to wait longer for or not acquire at all. It satisfies the desire for instant gratification and at the same time draws us smoothly into debt. Its purpose is to keep us under control and to make money for the company or individual offering the credit.

We are told in the Bible to be lenders rather than borrowers.[1]

The conditions under which we should lend are also given, along with the potential risks, if the interest charge is exorbitant.[2]

If we were to review the events which occurred in the Garden of Eden, we would soon see that God's plan for man was for him to have "fellowship" with God and enjoy all that He provided.[3] However, if we are to enjoy all that the Lord desires to give us for our use, then we are required to be diligent in obedience to His desires and careful to do His commandments.[4]

I remember when I was teaching in a secondary school, one student in particular, had come to me to ask for advice regarding a van he had purchased. The dealer had given credit to a student who worked part-time, so as to allow this student to purchase the van and carry a loan of $12,000.

This may not seem like much money, given today's prices, but this incident occurred in the mid-seventies. To me this seems unfair, as this student was in heavy debt before he even got started in a career. Obviously, he had to sell the van at a loss and pay off as much of the debt as possible, while settling the remainder from his part-time employment.

We are warned that being in "right standing with God" will not be without its struggle. He stated that the "thief" would come to steal, kill and destroy.[5] For many, financial freedom has given way to heavy debt which has killed our incentive, destroyed marriages and individuals, and stolen our hope for a comfortable future. This was not God's plan for our lives which He indicated when He said that He had come that we might have life and have it abundantly.[6] It should be noted that God not only states the requirements for our success, He also tells us that we do not have to wait until we die but that we can have that success now.[7]

To many, the requirements set out by God in His plan may seem harsh. Certainly, they call for discipline, accountability, and obedience. Adhering to this plan is not without its rewards by any means. For not only will we receive all good things during this lifetime on this earth, but we will receive life after this life.[8]

C. THE OTHER SIDE OF DEBT

Borrowing money from a friend, taking a bank loan, using a credit card, taking a mortgage and so on all adds up to one thing: debt. However, we might distinguish between debts that might be considered "good" and those that are otherwise.

For example, going into debt to purchase appreciating assets, such as a house, or borrowing money against your insurance to invest in something that will yield a higher rate of return than the interest being charged, may be considered a wise debt as well as wise stewardship. As an added bonus, the money borrowed to invest may be placed in an investment which is tax deductible.

Going into debt to invest in an appreciating asset is a skill that requires a disciplined investor. One who has experience and knows that there is a time to invest as well as a time to quit. He will also be well aware of what his total costs will be for the investment.

On the other hand, borrowing to finance a depreciating asset such as an automobile, pleasure boat or a recreational vehicle cannot necessarily be considered a wise investment or good debt. In some circumstances the credit card might be considered a good debt but on the whole this is not so. Even if we take advantage of the interest free loan period and make a point of paying everything outstanding on the due date, there is still the fact that, according to statistics, just having a credit card tempts us to spend more on average than someone who doesn't have a credit card and pays by cheque or with cash.

Hearsay suggests that someone using a credit card to make purchases and then paying the entire balance at month end will spend approximately 30% more than if they were using cash or cheques.

As we examine the steps to achieving financial freedom, we should bear in mind the world's plan and God's plan and their implications for our lives.

As you can see from the bar graph (Figure 1) illustrating the effect of compounding debt, if we were to borrow $1,000 at an annual rate of 16.5% we would incur interest of approximately $40.00 over a ninety day period. This means, in effect, that we are paying an effective daily interest rate of 17.9%.

INCREASING INTEREST ON UNPAID DEBTS

Calculated Annually At 16.5%

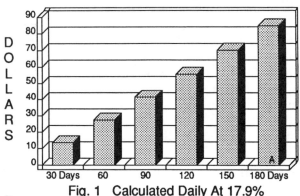

Fig. 1   Calculated Daily At 17.9%

Calculating The Cost Of Credit Cards

There are basically two types of credit cards; those issued by private organizations such as retail department stores, and those issued by financial institutions such as banks. While all lenders are now required to disclose how much interest is being charged for the use of credit, there is a difference in how the cost of credit is calculated. With the private companies, such as retailers, interest charges are normally calculated on the balance remaining in your account after any payment has been received and deducted from the previous balance. The typical bank card does not follow this practice. The banks normally charge interest on the full amount of your purchase back to either the date of your purchase or when they posted the amount to your account. This applies even if a partial payment is received.

The end result is that if you carry over an account balance from one month to the next, you would find a sizeable difference in the amount of interest you would be required to pay depending on which card you were using.

D. STEPS TO FINANCIAL FREEDOM

1. Freedom From Credit Problems

If you are serious about getting out of debt, the first step is to take action in the area of credit purchasing through the use of personal credit cards or accounts. Many individuals have accumulated so much indebtedness through credit cards that they can only meet the monthly minimum required payments. At that rate, the hole can only get deeper.

Steps to solving this problem:

a) **Stop** using credit cards. Better still, destroy them.

b) **Write** a letter to each of your creditors explaining what you and your spouse have agreed to do about the use of credit. Indicate your commitment to settling the debt and ask that your account be officially closed to any further use. Indicate in your letter that, in keeping with your budget, you will be making monthly payments of a specified amount of money until your account is settled. Phone each creditor and deliver this letter in person to their offices and solicit their support and co-operation.

c) **Return** any items which you or your family are now using and really do not need, requesting a refund or credit against your account. Remember, that if you have acquired debt for an asset that is appreciating in value, this represents good debt. However, to acquire debt for an asset that is depreciating in value is not good debt.

d) Seek professional help. Many municipalities provide credit counselling services. Check the Government listings in your area, if there is no services in your area, then consider seeking the help of a financial planner or other qualified professionals.

2. Self Portrait

This means taking a long hard look at the ways of the world and how we respond to them. It means looking at ourselves, too,[9] something we may find harder to do than taking a pair of scissors to our credit cards!

It is important that we recognize the ways of the world,[10] its manipulative ways and our susceptibility to them. Christians are told to be in the world but not of the world. We need to be aware of the psychological techniques that are brought to bear upon us, pressures to persuade us to conform and keep up with the "Jones", and live beyond our means.

For example, we live in a society where we have a tremendous amount of waste. It is a throw-away society. If we keep purchasing items that are not reusable, then we must replace the item at our expense. Large items cost large amounts of money and frequently put us in debt. Marketing strategies frequently include "building in" a planned obsolescence period for consumer goods. As a good steward, it is important for us to receive value for the dollars we spend.

As another example, it is common in most stores to place items near a cash register which may cause you to buy on impulse. These items are usually of low value but they account for millions of dollars in sales because this simple method is so very effective. Be aware of this scheme and resist it.

Another carefully planned strategy into which advertisers invest millions of dollars is to convince you that something you would like to have is not only something you want to have but something you actually **need**. Most of us, if not all, have wants.[11] It is the job of the advertising company to convince us not only that we cannot live without our want (that is, it is a need) but that our need can be met through credit purchasing. I wonder if you have a friend like George. George is an avid gardener who likes to purchase every type of tool available in the marketplace to support his hobby of gardening. George is always receiving something in the mail because he sends away for every new-fangled tool that has been offered on television.

The advertisers are usually successful at convincing him that he needs another new tool. George stores all these tools in his garden shed and for the most part is still paying for many of them. It is no surprise that he doesn't use many of them. He prefers to use the same old tools he's always used.

Now, God only agrees to supply our needs, not our wants, so it is our job to sensibly distinguish between what we want and what we, in reality, need. If we were to examine our property and its contents with a view to labelling "wants" and "needs", we would likely be surprised at the length of the first list as compared to the second. We shall deal with these items designated "wants" a little later in this chapter.

While in the marketplace, let's consider buying in general. The variety offered in any one item is frequently mind-boggling and, especially when time pressures us, or the salesperson assures us, "It's the best deal", we are tempted to buy rather than go to the trouble of checking around. This may be infuriating when we learn some time later that we could have made a better deal elsewhere!

We need to recognize our own weaknesses in the areas above and attempt to resist giving way to them.[12] In addition, here are a few tips to better make use of our money.

a) **Avoid impulse buying.** You may lose a few "good deals" this way but, by and large, you will avoid wasted expenditure.

b) **Consider the cost-benefit** of the item you are purchasing. Avoid products that are essentially throw-away and can only be used once or twice. Take the long term view and consider the replacement costs against purchase of a more lasting model.

c) Be sure to shop for the **best price** available. This means giving yourself time to compare, so plan ahead. Check out non-brand-name items that are recommended by consumer's guides.

d) Take advantage of **sales,** especially for end of season items. Keep a list of yearly events at which you can pick up bargains and pre-plan your attendance. Many department stores hold annual sales. Record the dates of these sales as they will likely repeat the same sale next year.

e) Use **coupons** whenever possible for items you need. Retailers are paid a handling fee, so they are happy to see you using them.

f) Leave your **check book** at home, if necessary, to control impulse buying and whenever possible shop from a pre-determined list.

g) Take time to evaluate, never rush a purchasing decision.

h) This policy works well; when in doubt, walk out.

3. Decisions For Lifestyle Changes

We Christians must apply discipline in our lives, even if it hurts for the moment.[13] Perhaps this discipline will be in the form of a sacrifice, such as increasing our giving or doing without something which we want, or think we need, or spending time with someone else instead of on ourselves.

This is the area that seems to hurt the most. It is difficult to change our lifestyle, even if the change is temporary. Most of us will remember Prime Minister Trudeau speaking on television when he would remind us to tighten our belts. He gave that speech so many times I felt that I went from a 38 to a 26 inch waist without a diet. But, it is good to re-examine our priorities, and, consequently, find that we are better off for making some needed change.

There are numerous areas which could be affected by such a review. For example, we might review our insurance needs, or re-consider our best option in the area of transportation needs and sell the second car. Perhaps we need to cut back on extravagant gifts and expensive vacations.

The cost of entertainment is often a major factor in our expenses. This includes both playing host in our homes and dining out or going to theatres and other places of entertainment.

If we are suffering from financial difficulties, entertainment is one of the principle areas to examine for possible expenditure reduction. We should consider alternate forms of entertainment involving self and family. For example, health is important. Consider a physical fitness program which you could do at home at a very reasonable cost.

When we want to save money and still allow ourselves the pleasure of entertainment at low cost, many of us decide to stay home and watch the television. I doubt very much whether this will save any money. In fact, I suspect that it will increase our spending. The reason: all those commercials that continue to bombard us with a lifestyle that we cannot afford. We see how the "other half" lives and we want to have the same things.

We might consider selling off all unnecessary assets such as a second car, boat and motor, camping trailer, motorcycle, furniture, stereo, television, video equipment and other like items. This may sound drastic, but in most cases these are the very items which put us in debt and in many situations there is more than one item per household. Use the funds to pay your creditors.

Also, consider selling the family home and moving to a less expensive home. Many cities offer comparable housing in the suburbs at a substantially reduced price. While commuting may increase your transportation costs, the saving may be much greater than the cost. If you own a cottage, summer home or have a time-share unit, you could consider selling these items and settling your debts.[14]

Decisions such as the above are of a major kind but may need to be made, if our desire for financial freedom is to be achieved.

As with all decisions, it is important to *involve the whole family* in the process. The same is true in deciding the areas of constraint.

It is essential for the family to conduct a meeting to determine what will be acceptable and what areas are forbidden. Adopting the idea of constraints is a positive step. For example, each member of the family might be allocated an allowance for the week which may be spent in any manner desired. However, there is no additional funding until the next allowance period. This is best determined during a budget session when each member of the family has an opportunity for input.

Since Bill and Flo are serious about getting out of debt, they will budget for only one family outing each week and perhaps eating out as a family only once a month. Of course, if it is only hamburgers and fries, maybe they could go more often.

Few Christians have a **written plan** or **clearly defined goals** and objectives for their lives. Goals and objectives are important, measurable guidelines that enable us to stay on track and know when we have completed a task. Imagine our state of panic if we were to fly across Canada with a pilot who does not have a flight plan, or is not able to tell us when we have arrived at our destination!

An astute Christian will always count the cost before beginning a project. It is prudent and wise to create a budget for the family to follow. The budget is a guide and lets us know when we are heading in the wrong direction.

It is most important for individuals to keep accurate and complete records of all financial transactions. It is very easy to fall into debt when you "think" you have the money to make a purchase. One family member should be in control of this area and all other members should consult this individual before a purchase.

4. Take Control For Success

The decisions that we make, the plans and budgets that we draw up should be designed to produce a positive cash flow. We must think positively in our financial planning.

Thinking positively means to think in terms of a **positive cash flow.** If we have more money coming into our possession than money leaving our possession, then we have positive cash flow. Conversely, a negative cash flow occurs when there is more money going out than coming in. If we have debts such that our entire payment is going to pay interest, we are in a negative cash flow position.

We cannot make progress in a deficit financing situation.

There has to be enough money available to meet our expenses. Only then are we in a position to put any left-over money to work.

A few dollars put in a savings account each week can mount up very quickly. See Figure 2.

Not only does such a deposit provide funds to draw on for a special occasion but it gives a feeling of satisfaction and visible proof that we are moving in the right direction.

As the situation improves, our thoughts should turn to better forms of investment for the future. These include market investments, retirement planning investments, estate planning and others.

48

SAVING ACCOUNT GROWTH

(Annual Deposit Of $1,500)

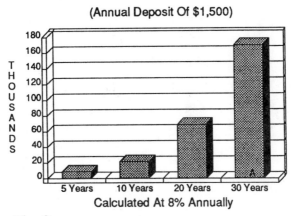

Calculated At 8% Annually

Fig. 2

One of the areas of investment that we as Christians should consider both for now and in the future is in the **area of tithing. Tithing is an important Christian responsibility.** If we truly understand the principles of giving and that God is the rightful owner of all we possess, then tithing is not only required, it is a joy to be able to participate. It is not the amount that is important but the principle. After all, God owns it all anyway! See Figure 3.

In all things, we as Christians are to put God first. The Bible states that God will supply all of our needs. We should seek the Lord and give Him an opportunity to become an active participant in our lives. Ask the Lord for advice; explain your needs to Him and truly seek His direction in all financial matters.

As we are expected to pay our taxes, we are also to pay back to God from that which He provides for us.[15] In this respect, we are also investing in His work and each tiny seed that is planted will have the opportunity to grow into greatness. If we are working in the Lord's will, under His direction, our efforts will not be wasted.[16]

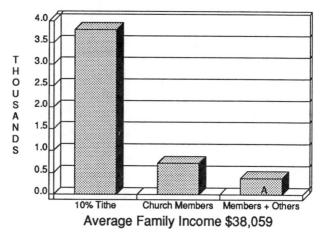

CHARITABLE GIVING IN CANADA 1985

THOUSANDS

4.0
3.5
3.0
2.5
2.0
1.5
1.0
0.5
0.0

10% Tithe   Church Members   Members + Others

Average Family Income $38,059

Fig. 3

E. SUMMARY

1. Credit Should Be Avoided
2. Consider Selling Unnecessary Assets
3. Consider Selling Real Estate Holdings
4. Limit And Change Methods Of Entertainment
5. Avoid Impulse Buying
6. Cut Down On Your Television Viewing
7. Avoid Products Which Will Become Obsolete Quickly
8. Think In Terms Of A Positive Cash Flow
9. Keep Accurate Records
10. Begin The Practice Of Tithing
11. Seek God's Counsel First
12. Prepare To Make Sacrifices
13. Prepare A Budget
14. Prepare A Written Plan
15. Begin Comparison Shopping

Things To Help Us Dig Out From Under

1. Of the two approaches to money management discussed (God's and the World's), identify the major points as they apply to your life.

2. What are the manipulative practices of the world that most affect you? (For example, do you always buy candy at the cash register?)

3. What is the total amount of interest you paid to creditors during the last year?

4. Over which areas of your lifestyle in money management do you most need to take control?

5. Take a sheet of paper and, by consulting your cheque book, charge card receipts or receipts from cash purchases, draw up a list of your spending for the most recent complete month. Separate these into two columns headed "Needed" and "Wanted". Examine the resulting total of each column. You may be surprised.

Chapter Four

Personal Planning Strategies

YOUR GOALS

At the close of this chapter, you will be able to:

a) identify the members of your planning team and their relative importance,

b) construct your own time frame to achieve previously determined goals and objectives; and

c) prepare your family budget.

A. INTRODUCTION

Just as Bill and Flo have done, this chapter allows you to use the information gathered previously to arrive at a financial plan for you and your family.

B. PUTTING YOUR PLANS INTO ACTION

Once Flo and Bill had determined just what their short and long term goals were, they were able to decide the means of reaching them. But, that is only part of the task they faced. Now they needed to establish how to put these plans in motion.

To do this requires team work and a carefully designed time frame in which to operate. Your team and your time frame are very personal to your particular needs. Nevertheless, there are certain basic considerations which Bill and Flo used in their situation.

C. DECISION MAKING:
WHO'S ON YOUR TEAM?

Just as it was for Flo and Bill, your team is made up of the following participants: The Lord, you and your spouse, then the remainder of your family, Christian counsel, Christian friends and various specialists. The normal tendency is to begin a personal financial plan without first consulting with the Lord. I feel that this is a mistake as He wants to be an active participant in all areas of our lives and should always be consulted first, regardless of the severity of the decision.

When I managed the financial planning department of a large international ministry, I recall a lady coming in for financial counselling. This lady was unemployed, a single parent, and was receiving social assistance. She had recently become a Christian and wanted to apply Christian principles in her life. She insisted on making a faith promise to give a large sum of money to charity. Frankly, I didn't think there was any way she could ever afford to donate to charity and still provide for her child.

Within a month, she returned to my office. She had found a job, was no longer receiving social assistance and had come to honour her pledge with a cheque for the full amount committed earlier. What happened? She began her journey back by starting with prayer. She committed her finances and her life to the Lord and asked for His help. When you and the Lord team up to do a job, even if the rest of the world opposes you, you will succeed. You and the Lord are a majority.

We are told that the Lord gives **wisdom** and that from him come **knowledge** and **understanding**.[1] We, as Christians, may receive these blessings, if we ask for them. First, though, we must have a right **attitude** toward the Lord. The fear (that is, reverence) of the Lord is the beginning of knowledge[2] and this, with the acceptance of these commandments in our lives, will enable us to seek and receive his counsel. When we acknowledge God in our lives and place our trust in Him, He will direct our steps.[3]

As with any team, the success desired is dependent upon all members understanding and doing their part to the best of their ability. This means we must communicate with each other. Each member is important and should have input in the process and this certainly applies to the Lord who should have the most important role. We know with certainty that the Lord is faithful[4] but He does require something from us. We must love Him and keep His commands. Then, like David, we can say, "I sought the Lord and He answered me, and delivered me from all my fears."[5]

In order to receive direction in our lives, financially or otherwise, we must be prepared to come to the Lord in prayer.[6] Prayer, unfortunately, seems to be a lost art to many Christians who don't really know how to pray nor, perhaps, believe in the effectiveness of prayer. Attaining effective prayer and success in financial planning have one ingredient in common: desire.

The fact that you are reading this book on financial planning shows that you have that desire to be effective in the area of your finances. Now we start to turn that motivation into productive activity.

D. GETTING STARTED

1. Bring In The Specialist

Many great and wonderful ideas lie dormant because some individuals thought that they had all the answers and didn't need any counsel. It is important in financial planning to **seek qualified help.** In some situations this help may be expensive but, in most cases, good, strong common sense is what is needed.

Solomon was a man of God, filled with wisdom and common sense. His teachings, that we must "listen to counsel and accept discipline, that you may be wise the rest of your days", have more direct application today than at any other time.[7] David stated that the counsel of the Lord never changes; that it stands **forever.**[8] Even so, he warns us that we must be careful of the counsel we seek, if we expect to receive His blessings.[9]

The Lord should be our first choice of counsel in any matter.[10] With His leading, we should seek the counsel of committed Christians who can often add that extra insight needed in a given situation.[11] For example, we may consult with our family, friends, and professional members of the body such as pastors, accountants, and financial planners.

With the help of these people, and through prayer, we can identify our needs and receive guidance in how to meet them. Figure 4 shows the relative importance of those who make up our team.

Fig. 4

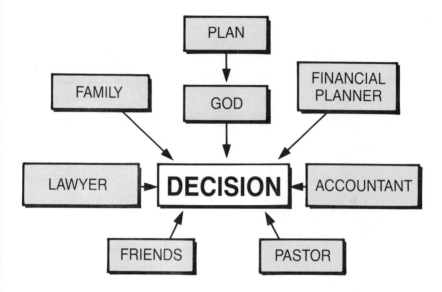

2. Preparing A Time Frame

Bill and Flo found it most helpful that they were able to decide when their plan would become active and when they could expect to complete it. It is important that the time frame you and your spouse select for implementing your plan has clearly marked points for applying and achieving your objectives. It is human nature to procrastinate and put off important and tough decisions. Unless we make a clear decision as to when to start and when to end, we are running the risk of never getting around to doing either.

To begin, refer to your prioritized short and long term goals and objectives. In order for you to measure your progress, it was necessary to designate a one year time period in which to accomplish your short term goals. The start up date for achieving your goals is not difficult; it is **NOW**

What requires careful consideration is the amount of time required for each objective. Do not condense the time frame so much as to put unnecessary stress or pressure on yourself to accomplish the objective.

Each of the prioritized goals and the possible three objectives for each goal will be transferred to a Personal Time Chart (found in the appendix) that will allow you to measure your progress.

Using Bill and Flo's sample Time Chart as a guide, enter your goals and objectives on your Personal Time Chart, found in the appendix.

SAMPLE TIME CHART

Name: **BILL & FLO**   Date: **1989**

	J F M A M J J A S O N D

1. Goal: Clear All Debts
Objective 1. Stop Credit Spending   ⊢————⊣
Objective 2. Write Creditors   ⊢—⊣
Objective 3. Prepare a Budget   ⊢—⊣

2. Goal: Begin Retirement Savings Program
Objective 1. Begin Saving   ⊢————⊣
Objective 2. Begin Course on Investing   ⊢——⊣
Objective 3. R.R.S.P.   ⊢—⊣

3. Goal: Children's Education
Objective 1. Begin A Saving Program   ⊢————⊣
Objective 2. Survey Other Parents   ⊢—⊣
Objective 3. Survey The Available Schools   ⊢————⊣

For example, Bill and Flo used this chart to focus on three special goals. The first was to clear all their debts. Their primary objective for this goal is to stop using their credit cards completely by the end of September. During January through May, Flo and Bill will write to their creditors and explain that they are intending to pay off and close their credit accounts completely and will not buy on credit again.

Also, during that period the entire family will sit down and prepare a budget so that by May they will be realistically budgeted for the rest of the year. It won't take long to do but they've vowed to do it before the end of May. From this chart you can see how they have decided to handle their other goals.

E. FREEDOM THROUGH THE FAMILY BUDGET

How many times have we sat down and written out a detailed budget to find that in a few short weeks or months we are not following anything contained in the budget? The reason for this usually resides in one or more of the following areas.

1. We do not really know how much money is coming in to the family and frequently we do not even know from which sources the money arrives. Bill and Flo don't have any secret sources of money but, sometimes, they have secret spending that they'll have to discuss now!

2. We have at best a poor idea (and usually no record) of where our money is being spent. The result is that we tend to spend beyond our limits and wind up in debt.

3. Our budgets are often so detailed and cumbersome that it will take too much time to keep current, so we procrastinate until the work load required to make our records current is an awesome task. Then we decide that we do not need a budget.

1. A Helpful Tool

A budget is a helpful tool and, more than that, it is a Biblical principle.[12] The purpose of the budget is to provide a guidance system that will send out alarm signals if we are heading in the wrong direction. It should not require more than approximately **thirty minutes a week** to update and report on your progress. If the budget becomes time consuming or burdensome, it is probably too detailed and should be refined.

Budgeting involves all family members. This includes its production and the commitment of all family members to live within the constraints discussed and agreed to by each family member. For some this may be difficult but determination and perseverance and commitment is all that is needed to make it work for you, rather than against you.

2. The Steps To A Successful Budget

a. Analysis Of Present Situation

We need to know where we are coming from before we can determine where we are heading. Review your Personal Asset Form completed in Chapter 2.

Remember that this document is an estimated picture of your entire estate at one particular point in time. We will be using some of the information from this form, in preparing your budget. In addition, I would recommend something which I do every year. I review all the cheques written on my account(s) during the past year. Then I categorize them into: utilities, rent, food, automobile expenses, insurance, department store expenditures, credit card purchases, loan payments and miscellaneous, etc. Then, I record the amount on a page like the one headed Analysis of Yearly Personal Spending which can be found in the appendix.

Next I indicate in the space beside the appropriate expenditure, where I think I might be able to make a reduction or where I would like my spouse to make a reduction. An important question to ask ourselves is this; does this expenditure satisfy our needs or our wants? If it satisfies only our wants, then there is likely room to make a reduction.

You can see Bill and Flo's analysis as an example to help guide you in areas where you might be able to make a change.

ANALYSIS OF YEARLY PERSONAL SPENDING

	Paid Out Last Year	Reduce Next Year
Cash Withdrawals	$ 800	$
Charitable Giving	75	
Rent/Mortgage	13,800	
Food	6,400	
Entertainment (Restaurants, Events, Etc.)	2,000	
Credit Card Payments	2,800	
Bank Loans	2,400	
Clothing Items	600	
Medical		
Utilities	1,200	
Telephone	475	
Vacations	1,000	
Personal Allowances		
Savings		
Transportation (Public, Car, Gasoline, Maintenance, Etc.)	2,500	
Home Improvements		
Unspecified Cash	2,800	
Miscellaneous	1,800	
TOTAL PAID OUT	$ 38,650	$

1. Did you receive lasting value for money paid out?
2. Did you indicate where you could reduce spending next year?

b. Sources Of Income

Complete the form title "Sources Of Monthly Income" by filling in the relevant blank spaces and use monthly figures where possible. If your income is weekly, then multiply by four and place in the appropriate space. Use your net salaries or "take home pay". See Appendix A for blank forms.

SOURCES OF MONTHLY INCOME	
	Amount
Present employment	$ _1833._
Spousal employment	_1250_
Part-time employment	
Investments	
Interest on money invested	
Money owed you/paid monthly	
Other	
TOTAL MONTHLY INCOME	$ _3083_

c. Fixed And Variable Expenses

The heart of budgeting is to determine which expenses are of a fixed nature (those that must be paid and do not vary in amounts) and those expenses which are variable (those that have no fixed payment or amount).

In monthly Fixed Expenses Flo and Bill list their typical fixed expenses but it may not be complete given your situation. Add or delete from the list until you have a personal and complete list of your fixed expenses.

Follow the same procedure for your Variable Expenses using the sheet provided in the appendix and personalize this list to cover your variable expenses.

We have included the tithe in the area of fixed expenses and would suggest that we are tithing on our **gross income,** not our net income.

61

MONTHLY FIXED EXPENSES

Amount

Tithe $ _____

Rent/Mortgage _**1150**_

Insurance _____

Bank Loans _**200**_

Health Insurance _____

Saving Program _____

TOTAL MONTHLY FIXED EXPENSES $ _**1350**_

MONTHLY VARIABLE EXPENSES

Amount

Food (At Home, Restaurants) $ _**700**_

Transportation (Ins., Gas, Fares _**210**_

Clothing _**50**_

Recreation _**70**_

Vacations _**83**_

Utilities (Heat, Hydro, Water) _**100**_

Home Improvements _____

Other _**659**_

TOTAL MONTHLY VARIABLE EXPENSES $ _**1872**_

d. Total Expenditures

Now we can combine our total fixed and variable expenses and place the figures on the page headed Monthly Income and Expenditures, found in the appendix.

MONTHLY INCOME AND EXPENDITURES	
Total Income	$ *3083*
Deduct: Total Expenditures	$ *3222*
NET BALANCES	$ *139.*

You have now accomplished the outline of your family budget.

While it is fragmented, you can pull all the sections together and transfer the information to the Family Budget Sheet.

However, you might want to review Figure 5. These will indicate the average percentage spent on each of the selected items across Canada as a total of family expenditures. This may help by serving as a guide when you complete your budget.

3. Preparing Your Budget

The Family Budget indicates your intended monthly expenses in various areas. It is this budget that will be your guide for future spending. See Figure 5.

SELECTED ITEMS AS AN AVERAGE
PERCENTAGE OF TOTAL FAMILY SPENDING

	Married Couple	Retired
Personal Taxes	19.8%	12.7%
Shelter (1)	16.6	20.8
Food	14.4	17.3
Transportation (2)	12.3	13.1
Household Operation	7.6	8.6
Clothing	6.4	5.0
Entertainment/Rec.	4.7	4.4
Security (3)	4.9	2.1
Miscellaneous (4)	3.9	2.6
Health/Personal Care (5)	3.8	4.5
Tobacco/Alcohol	2.8	3.0
Gifts/Contributions	2.7	5.9

(1) Includes property taxes, insurance, mortgages, repairs, utilities, etc.
(2) Includes public/private, airlines, automobiles, repair, etc.
(3) Includes life insurance, U.I.C., C.P.P., private/ government pensions.
(4) Includes interest, personal loans, tuition fees, union dues.
(5) Includes medical costs/insurance, cosmetics, personal care supplies.

Source: Stats. Can., Cat. 62-5555

Fig. 5

THE FAMILY BUDGET

INCOME	Monthly
Present Employment	$ 1833
Spousal Employment	1250
Part-Time Employment	
Investment Interest	
Canada Pension	
Old Age Security	
Private Pension	
Other	
TOTAL INCOME	$ 3083

EXPENSES	
Food	$ 500
Shelter	1000
Transportation	180
Entertainment	50
Recreation	
Security	100
Charitable Donations	483
Utilities	100
Taxes	150
Debt Payment	270
Investments	
Medical Expenses	
Clothing	50
Personal	
Other	50
TOTAL EXPENSES	$ 2883
SURPLUS CASH FLOW	150

4. Special Considerations

a. Discipline And Flexibility

In contrasting the athlete and the Christian "runner", Paul makes it clear that the key elements to success are **discipline** and single-minded **perseverance**.[13] Once we have made our commitment, we must be prepared to stick with it. Nevertheless, we must seek to avoid discipline that becomes burdensome and discipline that leads to failure to achieve goals.

All planning and subsequent goals and objectives should be subject to frequent review. If necessary, changes can and should be made during the process. For example, you may want to alter your goals, your objectives or your time chart by either adding or deleting from the original plan. As circumstances change, this may become a reality that cannot be avoided if the plan is not to become impossible to carry out.

While there is danger in becoming a slave to a time chart that is no longer appropriate given changed circumstances, there is also danger in modifying the time chart, deferring action that is needed, and so forth, if this is without good cause. Unwillingness to carry out appropriate objectives simply because of the effort required is not to be considered good cause. As in all decisions, modifications to our planning may be taken to the Lord for His direction.

F. SUMMARY

The personal commitment that you and your family bring to financial planning is crucial to its success or failure. Only direction from the Lord, as the most important member of your team of advisers, is more crucial. Good counsel is to be sought in all decision-making but, while discipline in adhering to these decisions is important, avoid being slavish to a plan that has been made redundant by changing circumstances.

What You Need To Know, To Know What You Need!

1. Why is it important to have qualified help in your financial planning decisions?

2. Which area of your budget will require the most scrutiny?

3. Who are the major participants on your team for managing your finances?

4. Focus on your answer to number two. Take a piece of paper and make a list of expenditures which can be avoided in the future. Circulate this list among the members of your family and seek their commitment to avoiding these unnecessary expenditures in the future.

Chapter Five

The Importance of Estate Planning

YOUR GOALS

At the close of this chapter, you will be able to:

a) explain the importance of a Christian Will,

b) identify the circumstances under which a Will is necessary,

c) evaluate your potential to do more for your family and charity through your estate plan,

d) complete a draft Will.

A. INTRODUCTION

Most Christians have not prepared any estate plans or, if they have, they probably have not considered the possibility of multiplying the effect of their gift to the Lord and their family.

B. A CHRISTIAN RESPONSIBILITY

1. The Importance Of A Christian Will

If we understand the Christian principle that God is the rightful owner of all that we possess[1] and that we are stewards (individuals loaned these things to manage for a short time), then it follows that we must be wise and manage well the things entrusted to us. This is because they were created by God and He has retained His ownership.[3]

Over a period of years, two interesting observations have been made to me; namely:

1. Christians who are in debt do not normally have a Will and those Christians who do not have a Will seldom get out of debt.

2. In Canada, approximately six to seven out of ten individuals have not prepared their Will.

From these observations, it is apparent that many Christians are not practising good stewardship. We read in the Bible that we should honour the Lord from our wealth and from the first of all our produce.[4] Our wealth is that amount which we have accumulated over the years and are now using as we determine. This wealth is composed of our investments, our houses, our summer homes, our recreational equipment, and many other possessions. When we prepare a Will that honours the Lord with a gift, we are acknowledging His rightful ownership of our wealth.

Procrastination is likely the chief reason, if not the only reason, that most Christians have not prepared their Will. Our lifestyles are accelerating at such a pace that we barely have enough time to accomplish the things we must do apart from the things we would like to do.

Yet, it is the **responsibility of every Christian** to manage these matters for our Master.[5] We also read that if anyone does not provide for his own, and especially for those of his household, he has denied the faith and is worse than an unbeliever.[6]

2. Why Have A Will?

A **Will is necessary for all Christians** as it enables them to help satisfy their responsibility of being a faithful steward.

In addition, it alleviates potential conflict within the family as our loved ones try to determine how we might have wanted to disperse our assets.

The difference between a Christian and non-Christian Will is that the Christian Will honours the Lord with a gift to carry on His work. This enables the Church and various ministries to carry out their mandate and in proper time reap a harvest.[7]

If we were to die intestate (without a Will), the various organizations which we supported in life, as well as our friends and relatives, might not receive a gift. If they were to receive a gift, it may not be in what we would consider the proper proportion and thus others might receive more than those who have the greater need.

The use of a Will enables us to make a gift to the Lord without putting ourselves in any present financial hardship. As well, the use of a Will allows us to know that we can continue to participate in the work which we supported during our life, after we have gone to be with the Lord.

A Christian Will simply means that we can control and disperse our assets, accumulated over a lifetime, the way we want and not the way the Provincial Law would dictate if we did not have a Will. A Christian Will also allows us to control the receipt of funds so that an inheritance is not fully spent, often within six months, on foolish items.

Our Will enables us to appoint guardians to take care of our minor children or our disabled relatives and friends. Without this provision the Province would likely appoint someone or an organization to manage these and other financial affairs for us.

Certainly, one of the benefits which we can include in our Will is the opportunity to take advantage of tax planning regulations in effect at the time we are writing or revising our Will. This would allow us to render to Caesar what is Caesar's and to God what is His[8].

3. Who Should Prepare Our Wills?

A Will document is legal and binding and should not be prepared by an amateur. Simply stated, it is not wise to make your own Will without consulting a lawyer. A number of individuals will not want to use a lawyer because they perceive that the experience will be costly in time and money. The result is procrastination....sometimes for too long.

I met a lady who was seventy-five years young, living alone in an apartment in downtown Toronto. This very kind lady decided that it was about time that she prepared her Will and put her financial affairs in order. I was delighted to assist her, and it didn't take very long. Our meeting was in mid December and her appointment to see her lawyer for the final signing of her Will was on January, 6. This dear lady wanted to leave some money to her close, life long friends, as well as a distant niece. Unfortunately nothing was ever accomplished. She died on January 3 and she died intestate. Her intentions were not enough. She simply waited too long.

Frequently, in do-it-yourself Wills, important information which should be included in the Will is left out of the document because we are not familiar with Canadian law and in some situations the Will is not binding. We have achieved the same results as if we had died intestate, just because we tried to save time or money.

It is **wise stewardship** to prepare ourselves by consulting with a financial planner before we visit our lawyer. The financial planner explains the various terms which will be used and helps us to understand their meaning. Such a professional has much experience in situations like ours and can offer good suggestions that may benefit us greatly.

Financial planners work closely with our lawyers to help ensure that our wishes are carried out by the lawyer. However, the lawyer is ultimately responsible for the final draft of your Will.

4. When Do We Need A Will?

If we do not have a Will at present, then we are likely in need of one. It is not a matter of how much money we own or how many assets we possess, but rather what we are doing with the assets which are now in our estate. We must prove ourselves faithful with a little before the Lord will give us more.[9]

Many Christians have carried out their responsibility and prepared a Will. Some may have prepared their Wills years ago and have it tucked away in a safety deposit box. Even though they have already prepared a Will, it may need to be revised. Our views and thoughts are constantly changing and a Will should reflect our **current** thinking and desires.

It would be wise to talk with a financial planner if any of the following circumstances apply to you:

    a) You have no Will.
    b) You were recently married.
    c) You were recently divorced.
    d) Your Will is three years old or more.

e) You are a recent widow or widower.
f) You have not prepared a Christian Will.
g) Your Will does not reflect your current thinking.
h) You have received a large inheritance.
i) You are a new parent.
j) You have had a major change in your finances.

5. Increasing Our Effectiveness

Increasing our effectiveness is a fundamental desire of most Christians. To be able to provide a gift to the charity of your choice, as well as make provisions for our own family is extremely important.[10] It certainly is a comfort for us to know, that with God nothing is impossible[11] and that He is able to do immeasurably more than we could ask or imagine.[12]

Many Christians forget that we must effectively use what we have before God will give us an increase.[13]Therefore we must learn to be good managers of the resources God has given us, especially if we desire to manage more as it is indicated we can in the parable of the talents.[14]

When asked, Christians generally respond with a resounding "yes" to the idea that they could make a substantial gift to charitable work and still provide the financial security that they desire for their family. This may be achieved through proper estate planning that enables us to make that substantial gift and at the same time provide financial security for our family.

We must commit ourselves to the terms and conditions outlined in the Bible, if we expect God to give us His blessing. We are to seek Him and His righteousness[15]and take authority and possess His blessing.[16] For it was God who said:

> Let Us make mankind in Our image, after Our likeness; and let them have complete authority over the fish of the sea, the birds of the air, the beasts, and over all the earth, and over everything that creeps upon the earth. (Ge.1:26, Amp.Ver.)

Outlined on the following pages are some flow charts which show the possible effectiveness of various estate planning concepts.

The Traditional Plan outlines a Simple Will which is not designed to multiply the effects of the estate. This Will is often referred to as an "I love You" Will. Mom leaves everything to Dad and Dad leaves everything to Mom. When both parties have "passed away" the children receive what is left in equal shares.

It is worth noting that the American national average suggests that the inheritance is fully spent in less than 6 months. It is not likely that this figure would change any here in Canada. Imagine working for forty years to have the entire lifetime accumulations spent in less than six months. Fortunately, something can be done about this possible situation.

The Traditional Plan With A Gift To Charity illustrates the same Simple Will, only there is a special gift to charity and your estate would receive a tax credit for the gift. As before, the inheritance is divided equally among the children.

The Traditional Plan Maximizing Our Giving offers the opportunity for a larger gift to your family as well as a larger gift to charity. For ease of illustration we have not shown any possible tax consequences, as tax may or may not be payable depending on how investments have been arranged.

When both husband and wife have "passed away" the money is placed in a special trust fund. The income earned on the money held in this trust fund is paid out to your heirs and/or charity until the total money paid out equals the original investment. At this point the original investment could be divided anyway you want. This type of plan offers much to those of us who would like to teach their children how to manage money. As well, we are able to continue to participate in the charities we supported during our lifetime.

Fig. 6

TRADITIONAL PLAN

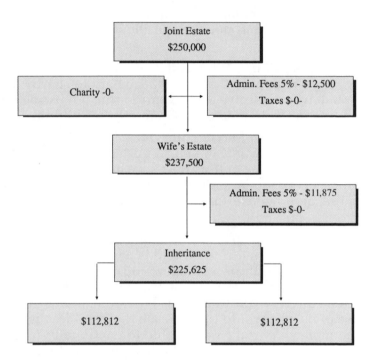

Results:

1. Children receive $225,625
2. Charity receives -0-
3. Deductions $24,375
4. American national average: Inheritance **spent in 6 months.**

Fig. 7

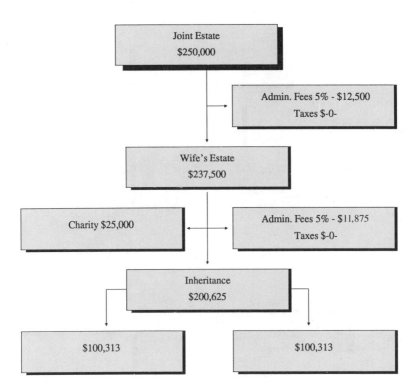

**TRADITIONAL PLAN
WITH GIFT TO CHARITY**

Joint Estate
$250,000

Admin. Fees 5% - $12,500
Taxes $-0-

Wife's Estate
$237,500

Charity $25,000

Admin. Fees 5% - $11,875
Taxes $-0-

Inheritance
$200,625

$100,313

$100,313

Results:

1. Children receive $200,625
2. Charity receives $25,000
3. Deductions $24,375
4. American National Average: Inheritance **spent in 6 Months.**

75

Fig. 8

TRADITIONAL PLAN
MAXIMIZING OUR GIVING

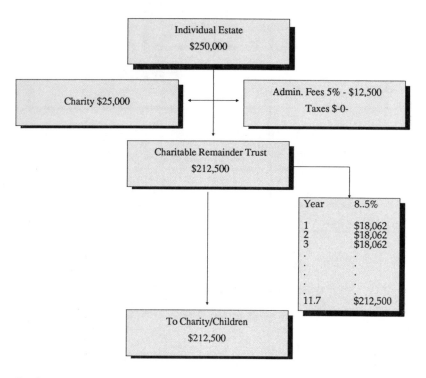

Results:

1. Continue to participate in charity
2. Help assure ongoing programs
3. Provide yearly gift $18,062
4. Total gift to Charity/children $450,000
5. Stabilizes Charitable growth

6. Power of Attorney

At some point in our life, it would be wise to consider giving a close family member "Power Of Attorney" to act on your behalf. In the event of an accident or a serious medical problem, immediate action could be taken to provide necessary care. This is a subject you should discuss with your lawyer and family members.

C. STEPS IN PREPARING OUR CHRISTIAN WILL

Preliminary Steps:

In order for us to be aware of how well the Lord has provided for our needs, we would suggest the following:

   a) Review your net worth, from your Asset Summary Sheet in Chapter 2.

   b) Review the goals you and your spouse determined as your top three priorities in Chapter 2.

At this point, Bill and Flo have decided to prepare a draft outline of their Will in order to prepare for their meeting with their lawyer. They will do this by answering the questions that follow. They are always in control of their Will and they are able to make changes whenever they desire.

In order to be better prepared when they meet their lawyer Bill and Flo answered the following points.

1. Appointment of Executor/Executrix

Determine who you would like to be your executor or executrix of your estate. Consider an alternate choice. You can select more than one person to represent you, if you desire. Executors are allowed to charge a fee for their services which could cost as much as 5% of the probated estate. For this reason, you may want to consider a family member for this position. Once you have decided on your executor/ executrix notify the person and ask if they would accept the position and either give them a copy of your Will or tell them where it may be located.

Bill and Flo have made an inventory of their assets as well as a list of their professional advisors, bank accounts, and ivnvestments so that nothing will be missing when it is time to settle their estate.

2. Guardian For Minor Children

This next step is an important one; the selection of a guardian of minor children. It should be noted that indicating your choice of a guardian does not guarantee that your wishes will be met. However, in all likelihood, your choice of a guardian will be upheld.

3. Last Statement Of Charitable Intent

Determine what percentage you and your spouse would like to leave to charitable work. In addition, consider where you want your funds to go and how the funds will be used. You are investing the Lord's money, so get the best return for your dollar. Remember to consider your church and ministries which you have supported during your lifetime.

4. Selective Distribution To The Children

You may wish your estate to be divided among your children either in equal or unequal amounts. Discuss the needs of your children with your spouse and find some agreement as to what you desire to do for your children. Large sums of money received as an inheritance can cause people to change. Also, you may wish to put the inheritance in trust prior to dispersment at a later time.

5. What About My Friends?

This is your estate plan and you can do whatever you want to do with any part and/or all of it. You may chose to leave a gift to special friends, distant relatives, you are always in control of your estate.

D. MEANWHILE . . . SOUTH OF THE BORDER!

Charitable giving in the United States is alive and well. Americans are very generous people. In 1986, charitable gifts and bequests by individuals exceeded $77 billion. I am sure that much of this generosity is motivated by the substantial tax advantages gained from gifts.

It was Congress, who in 1917, provided for favourable tax treatment of charitable contributions by individuals, who are the primary source of charitable giving.

For many Americans, the federal income tax is the major item in the budgets of most taxpayers. Therefore, it is a natural consequence for individuals to seek counsel in the area of tax planning.

1. Current Giving

Current gifts are the most common type of gift. These are outright gifts of money or other assets owned by an individual. Because this is the most common, the tax planning associated with this type of giving is usually straightforward, but there are times when it can become complicated depending on the property given to charity as well as the timing of the gift.

There are limitations on the amount that can be deducted in any one year. The limitations are based upon the donor's "contribution base." This "contribution base" is determined through an adjusted gross income. The limitations may be 50%, 30% or 20% of the base. The amount depends upon the status of the organization as well as what type of gift you are planning to contribute.

Experience has shown that tax planning is necessary if tax benefits of current gifts are not to be deferred or lost through the various percentage limitations. Proper planning may ensure a deduction for the full value of the gift.

2. Deferred Giving

When we speak of deferred giving, we are referring to a donor who makes an irrevocable gift of a future interest in property to a charity. The reason that it is deferred is that the donor continues to use and enjoy the gift now, and in many cases, receives a current income tax deduction now. The gift may pass to the charity at either a specified future date or upon the death of the donor. This means that the donor has increased his cash-flow from use of the current deduction.

Deferred giving requires the use of a specialist to ensure that the donor receives maximum benefit from the gift. Wisdom would dictate that anyone desiring to plan a deferred gift should seek out a qualified estate planning attorney, for advice.

American law permits the use of many instruments such as Charitable Remainder Trusts. These trusts may be either a Charitable remainder annuity trust or a Charitable remainder unitrust. In a charitable annuity trust the specific distribution from the trust must be a certain sum and cannot be less than 5% of the initial fair market value of the trust assets. However, in the situation where there is a unitrust, the specific distribution must be a fixed percentage which is not less than 5% of the value of the trust assets calculated each year.

The Charitable lead trust can be very beneficial, depending upon the intent and desires of the donor. This allows for funds to be placed in trust and the income earned paid out each year. It is called a lead trust because the charity leads with the income paid to the charity and the residue passed along to the heirs several years later. This can achieve a substantial reduction in the amount of estate tax.

Charitable Gift Annuities are a very common form of making a charitable gift. The donor will purchase an annuity contract from a charitable organization for more than its market value. The difference between the price paid and the market value becomes a gift to the charity, which is tax deductible in the year the gift is made.

E. SUMMARY

You are now in a position to have this information presented to a Christian lawyer for the preparation of your Will. It is most important for the protection of your family and accomplishments of your goals that you **do not delay** this part of your financial plan.

Avoiding Procrastination

1. Make a list of the various items your lawyer would want to discuss with you pertaining to your estate plan.

2. Prepare a complete list of all of your assets, legal papers, professional advisors, investments and notify your executor/executrix of the location of this list.

Chapter Six

Tax Planning Strategies

YOUR GOALS

At the close of this chapter, you should be able to:

a) distinguish between tax evasion and tax reduction

b) identify the professional best suited to help you in your area of taxation; and

c) identify areas that could be applied to your income to allow for tax reductions.

A. INTRODUCTION

Tax Planning is important, as it may allow for reduced taxes, enabling you to provide more for your family now and in the future. Tax Planning is good stewardship and should be practised by all Christians. Tax regulations are constantly changing and while we have suggested a few ideas in this chapter which we anticipate will be available, we cannot be sure that they won't be changed. It is for that reason that we urge you to consult with your accountant or other professional advisor before implementing any of the ideas in this chapter.

B. CREATIVE TAX PLANNING

1. Biblical Principle

The Bible teaches Christians to be good citizens and pay their taxes.[1] There is a difference between tax reduction and tax evasion. The latter is illegal and the former is good stewardship. When we speak of creative tax planning we are speaking of tax reduction.

In Canada, we pay a number of taxes at various levels in the product life cycle. You and I pay taxes at the wholesale level and again at the retail level, as well as through our income deductions at source, each pay period.

Many Christians see as their goal, a desire to pay the minimum amount of tax legally owing, and nothing more. In order to accomplish this, we may need some creative tax planning. Creative tax planning starts with our using an accountant. The reason that many of us do not use an accountant is because we fear the cost involved. We should not[2] for experience has indicated that using someone who is a specialist in a given area not only saves time, and money, but it is done right the first time. The accountant is a specialist who frequently saves enough money for us through proper planning that he pays for himself in almost every situation.

I strongly recommend that Christians seek the advice of a Christian accountant in the preparation of their income tax and other tax planning matters in order to avoid paying unnecessary taxes. The need for proper tax planning is confirmed by the size of our household incomes. See Figure 9 which indicates the average family income in Canada for the year 1985. Note that the income is higher in Ontario than any other area of Canada. Can we really afford to not seek professional help?

FIGURE 9 goes here

CANADIAN AVERAGE FAMILY INCOME

1985

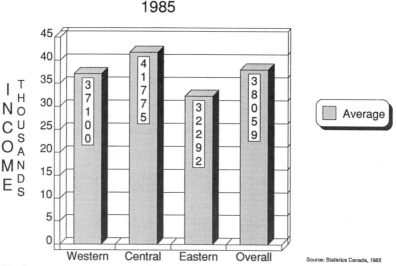

Fig. 9

Source: Statistics Canada, 1985

C. TAX STRATEGIES

1. Deferring Taxes Through Your RRSP

It is important to take advantage of the current limits allowing for the establishment and funding of your own RRSP. Monies placed into your retirement plan can grow very quickly. For example, $1,000 dollars placed into your RRSP each year for twenty years, earning 10% interest, would generate a fund in excess of $63,000. In addition, we would also have a tax deduction each year which would generate a tax refund. Everyone should have an RRSP. Your RRSP could very well be your only source of income in retirement.

Under the new rules of Tax Reform, Canadians who are solely dependent upon their RRSP contributions for retirement income, will see the dollar contribution increased. All taxpayers will have the right to carry forward any unused RRSP contribution for a period of seven years.

Two of my favourite words are "tax-deductible". The only two words that sound better than tax-deductible are "tax-free". The RRSP allows us to enjoy all four of these words. We are permitted under law, to enjoy tax-free compounding of our tax-deductible contributions to our RRSP, as long as the money remains in our retirement plan. This means we have more dollars compounding, and we end up with more when the plan is utilized in our retirement.

Your RRSP offers flexibility. Unlike a company pension, which you receive when you retire at age 65, the start-up of your pension using your RRSP could be delayed until the end of the year in which you turn seventy-one. This is important because the longer you can defer receiving payments from your RRSP, the longer the money can accumulate tax-free, (I like those words), and the more money you will have in your retirement.

Remember that this money will be taxable when it is withdrawn from your retirement plan. But since your major source of income will stop or be reduced, these funds will likely be taxed at a lower rate than when they were first deposited in your account.

2. Charitable Donations

Many Canadians do not give any money to charity. This is unfortunate for both the charity and especially the potential donor. When I think of the thousands of people I have met who give to their church, support other ministry work, as well as make donations to the public sector, I think of some of the most content and happy people I know. There is real joy in giving, and it belongs to the one who gives. It is not related to the size of the gift, but rather the intent of the gift.

Both Canadians and Americans rely heavily on the important contribution made by the voluntary sector of their respective countries. Equally, the volunteer community must rely on the charitable donations from all of us, to support its good work.

As a result of tax reform, those who give more will receive the greatest tax assistance. We will be given a tax credit which will reduce taxes directly and give everyone the same amount of tax credit for the same size of charitable gift.

CHARITABLE GIVING IN CANADA 1985

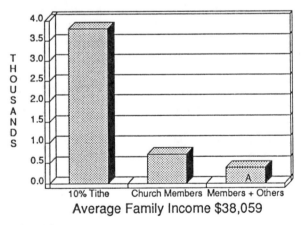

Average Family Income $38,059

Fig. 10

Charitable giving can have a significant impact on your income taxes. Any excess donations made in any one year can be carried forward for five years. As well, donations made in a particular year do not need to be claimed. If this happened to be a low income year and you knew next year would be better, you might choose to hold those tax receipts and apply them next year or in any of the following five years.

The taxation statistics for 1982 indicate that the average gift to charity per taxpayer, based on their assessed income (not the gross income), was $130.00 per year. This represents approximately 0.53% of our taxable income. Evidently, there is much room for improvement.

The Christian tends to give far more (approximately 2%) than this amount but still appears to fall short of giving a tithe (10%). Based on the 1986 Church Financial Statistics for twenty-seven Canadian Church bodies, with population exceeding 3.87 million, Christians gave per capita $208.03. Refer to Figure 10 and Figure 11.

Surely we could do much more for our favourite charities when you consider that many individuals will go to a restaurant and enjoy a fine meal and pick up the bill for our friends..... then leave a gratuity of ten to fifteen percent.

CHARITABLE GIVING IN CANADA
Summary Statistics Of Church Finances 1986

		Confirmed Membership	Inclusive Membership*	National Avg. Income (1985)	Tithe 10%
	Churches				
Denominations	27	$388.72	$208.03	$38,059	$3,806
Membership	(2.08M)	(3.89M)	(Family)	(Family)	
Family Gifts		$777.44	$416.06		
Percentage of income		2.04%	1.09%		

*Inclusive membership refers to those who are full, communicant, or confirmed members, plus other members baptized and adherents.

Source: Journal of Stewardship. Commission On Stewardship, New York, 1988.

Fig. 11

3. Moving Expense

If you are moving your residence to take up a new job, and your move is closer to your new employment by 40kms., your expenses are deductible from your personal taxes. This includes the moving company, storage, and, if you are forced into temporary lodging, accommodation and food.

Real estate and legal fees may also be deductible. You will need to produce receipts with your tax return, in order to qualify for these deductions.

4. Interest Compounding

Beginning January 1, 1988, interest earned and received in the year is fully taxable.

Compounding interest generates more money in your pocket because you are earning interest on your interest. This is only available for a period of three years at which time you must declare all the interest earned and pay your taxes.

However, money placed into your R.R.S.P. will earn interest which can be compounded until you withdraw the funds, at which time the money received is taxable. An alternative to interest-bearing investments is to place money into a capital gains situation such as real estate, mutual funds or stocks. These investments allow the first $100,000 worth of capital gains to be received tax-free. After reaching this level, you will still be taxed at a reduced rate.

RRSP POTENTIAL GROWTH

Requires $2,000 Deposit Annually

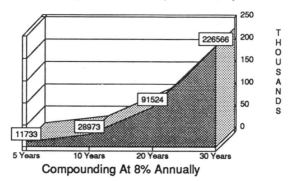

Compounding At 8% Annually

5. Mortgages

Many home owners have a mortgage which will be renewable within five to ten years, depending upon the length of term of the mortgage. When renewing your mortgage, consider increasing the frequency of payments and moving from a mortgage that is now paid monthly, to one paid weekly or bi-weekly. This can save a large sum of money by reducing the number of years of amortization.

For example, assume that you have a mortgage of $50,000 and a constant mortgage rate of 11%. The cost and the savings of paying your mortgage more frequently is indicated in Figure 9.

a. Write-Off Mortgage Interest

Many individuals have managed to purchase a home and in most situations the home has a mortgage. Unfortunately, we are not allowed to deduct the interest we pay to the mortgage company from income tax in the usual way.

Generally speaking, interest charges on money we borrow to make investments which have the potential to offer a reasonable profit are tax deductible. We can use this idea to our advantage if we have some investments.

One route to take is to sell the investments to make a payment on or eliminate your mortgage (to "pay it down"). This saves a considerable dollar amount in interest on your mortgage; interest that is not tax deductible.

The next step is to borrow enough money to purchase or re-purchase your investments. The interest on this loan is tax deductible at the present time. The home may be used as security to borrow the investment capital. Because you are borrowing funds to make an investment with a "reasonable expectation of profit," the interest charges are now tax deductible.

MORTGAGE COMPARISON CHART

Repayment Plan	Payments Frequency	Interest Cost	Paying Years	Interest Savings
Monthly	12	$94,373	25	-0-
Biweekly	26	$63,199	18.1	$31,174
Weekly	52	$62,845	18.0	$31,528

Source: TD Bank, Toronto, 1987

There's bound to be broker's fees involved and, of course, you risk changes in the market between divesting and subsequent re-investing but the long term savings can be considerable. Even if you do not have enough money able to eliminate your mortgage it would be wise to pay down your mortgage as much as possible.

b. Making Money Through Your Mortgage

If you have been contributing to an RRSP for sometime, you could have the potential to increase the growth of your retirement savings program. Let's assume that you have approximately $30,000 to $50,000 in your RRSP. By maintaining a self-directed RRSP you could invest in a mortgage held on your home.

Each month, you would make payments to repay the loan, just as you would if you were dealing with a large financial institution. The difference is that you are now earning the money inside your RRSP, which is accumulating at an accelerated rate, and, if you use the proceeds for other investments inside the RRSP, then you may be in a position to claim deductions for the interest payments associated with your mortgage.

There is a double benefit to be gained. We are able to contribute up to the maximum allowable yearly contribution to our RRSP as well as an additional contribution through mortgage payments and possibly receive tax reductions through the RRSP and the interest on the mortgage.

There are some costs and rules involved in this type of transaction. First, you must charge yourself a competitive mortgage rate. That is to say, you must be in line with the rates charged by other lenders. Second, there are the usual administrative and legal fees which pertain to mortgages and self-directed RRSP's. You are placing yourself in the position of wearing two hats; one as a lender and the other as a borrower.

You will have to pay a mortgage setup fee and mortgage insurance as well as appraisal fees on your property. In addition, the yearly fee for a self-administered RRSP is likely to be higher when its connected with a mortgage. One important requirement in an arrangement like this is that the mortgage has to be on your principal residence, which means you cannot go this route on investment property.

Finally, if you are switching your mortgage from some other lender to lend to yourself, you may find that you face discharge fees, which could be quite expensive.

Although this may deter many from this arrangement, a little perseverance could pay large dividends.

This idea will also benefit those who do not have enough money to assume the entire mortgage. Consider applying the same principles and take on a second mortgage on your home. This will still provide a substantial contribution to your retirement fund.

c. Saving Money Through Your Mortgage

Mortgages are, of course, drawn up to benefit the lender, principally. There may be certain advantages over one mortgage or another in terms of interest rates and shorter loan periods but the traditional mortgage amortized over 25 years at an interest rate in excess of 10% gives the borrower few benefits.

In such a loan, Bill and Flo, may find that they are "locked-in" for quite awhile. The loan is arranged so as to balance interest and principal so that the monthly payment remains the same over the period of the mortgage. At 11% compounded semi-annually and amortized over 25 years, this monthly payment is $1,155.04 on a principal of $120,000. At the end of five years, therefore, the mortgagee has paid $69,302.40, of which $6,275.49 has gone to reducing the principal. At this point the balance due, with interest, will be $114,879.55. The point is, that Bill and Flo will make payments of nearly $70,000 over five years and have reduced the money owing by little more the $5,000! By the time they pay off the mortgage at the end of the twenty five year period they would have paid for it 3 or 4 times over.

Generally, lenders will allow payments of extra monies against the mortgage once a year on the anniversary date. Some mortgages are completely closed and do not allow this; others stipulate a percentage of the outstanding principal as the maximum lump sum payment.

For example, a lump sum payment of $827 one year into our mortgage of $120,000 at 11% would result in a saving of interest charges of just over $9,500. Extra money paid at the end of the first year has saved you twelve months of interest payments. So, in most situations, homeowners who have a mortgage would do very well if they were to invest in their own mortgage. Most mortgages allow for a prepayment each year and some of these prepayments can be as high as fifteen percent of the principal.

6. Did You Say.....Not Taxable?

Many individuals are in such a hurry to pay their income tax each year, that they frequently pay tax on money which the government has declared is non-taxable income. Although it may not appear to be a tax planning strategy, paying tax only on taxable income is wise planning.

The following are a few examples where we might save a few dollars as these items are designated non-taxable income. Note that we are only suggesting a few items for your consideration and would recommend that you discuss your areas of concern with your accountant.

a) **Inheritance Money**
   Although the estate of the deceased may have to pay some tax, depending on how funds are held, money received through an inheritance is considered to be tax-free.

b) **The Lottery**
   Many individuals spend money on lottery tickets each week. For those very few who win, their prize is received tax-free. When this income is invested to earn additional income, then the income from the investment becomes taxable.

c) **Insurance**
   If you purchased insurance to provide an income in the event of an illness, the proceeds from your policy may not be taxable. The stipulation is that the insurance must have been paid by you, and the policy purchased by you, without any involvement by your employer.

   If you received insurance or a settlement from the Worker's Compensation Board because of an injury received while at work, these funds are non-taxable.

d) **Benefits Received From Your Employer**
   The benefits enjoyed by an employee, where there may be a discount applied to purchasing merchandise from

the employer, are not regarded as taxable benefits. This also applies to subsidized meals provided by an employer so long as the employee is charged a reasonable amount. If your employer requires you to use the local transit system for deliveries or other errands you may be given a monthly transit pass. You may use this pass as often as you like and it is considered non-taxable.

e) **Family Allowance Cheques**
When you place the family allowance cheque into a savings account for the benefit of your child, the bank will send you a T5 information slip. The banks do this because the child is a minor. Many times the mother adds this amount to her income and pays tax even though she is not required to include this in her taxable income. For the most part, a child can earn several thousands of dollars and pay no tax.

D. TAX REFORM

1. Major Highlights

(as outlined in the White Paper presented June, 1987 and ammended in December, 1987).

a) The number of tax categories will be reduced from 10 to 3, effective for 1988.

b) The current 3% now charged as a federal surtax will continue until the new sales tax reform is in place.

c) The federal tax rate applied to taxable income over $55,000 will be the top rate at 29%. This is a reduction from 34%. When combined with the provincial tax rate in Ontario, this gives a combined rate of 44.81%.

d) Personal exemptions and other deductions will be changed from a series of deductions against taxable income to a credit against the tax payable.

e) Contributions to R.R.S.P.s will not be phased in as quickly as previously announced. The limits for the 1987 tax year will remain at a maximum of $7,500 and the same in 1988. Following 1988 the limits will be raised until we reach the new maximum of $15,500 in 1995 and the plan will be indexed thereon.

f) The employment expense deduction has been eliminated as has the interest and dividend deduction of $1,000, effective 1988.

g) The maximum lifetime capital gains exemption has been reduced to $100,000.00, although it may be more. Best to see your accountant if this applies to you.

h) Effective in 1988 and subsequent years the charitable donations will be calculated on the basis of a tax credit and not the tax deduction. Charitable donations will be given a federal credit of 17% of the first $250 and 29% credit for donations in excess of $250. The amount qualifying for the credit will be restricted to 20% of your net income. **Unused donations may be carried forward up to five years.**

i) Medical Expense Deductions: Deductions for medical expenses are being converted to a 17% credit of the amount by which eligible expenses exceed either $1,500 or 3% of net income, whichever is less.

j) Tuition Fees: Students will be allowed a credit of 17% of post-secondary tuition fees. As well, a further $10 per month credit may be claimed when in full-time attendance at college or university.

k) Interest and Dividend Income Deduction: The $1,000 interest and dividend income deduction is gone.

R.R.S.P. YEARLY CONTRIBUTION LIMITS

The contribution limitations will be phased in on a slower plan than previously announced by the government. The phasing in of the new limits will be as follows:

Year	Amount
1988	7,500
1989	8,500
1990	10,500
1991	11,500
1992	12,500
1993	13,500
1994	14,500
1995	15,500

E. SUMMARY

As we have seen, attention to our taxes, particularly in the area of deferrals, is good common sense. My experience has shown me that this is not an area where the average individual feels comfortable. That is why I want to remind everyone that it is wise planning to obtain the advice of a professional. Furthermore, it is important to bear in mind that we are not only deferring income now but planning for the future of our entire family.

Important Questions

1. Explain the difference between tax reduction and tax evasion.

2. Which professionals are best qualified to help you in your tax planning strategies?

3. What tax reducing areas are most useful to you at this time?

4. Contact the Department of Finance, Tax Reform, 140 O'Connor Street, Ottawa, Ontario, K1A 0G5, and request information about tax reform.

5. Evaluate your RRSP and from discussion with various lending institutions determine if you would benefit from funding your own mortgage.

6. Evaluate what effect a doubling of your charitable contributions would have on your taxes. Use last year's tax return as a guide. If you have not given to charity resolve to make a contribution this year and increase each subsequent year.

Chapter Seven

Planning For Retirement

YOUR GOALS

At the end of this chapter, you should be able to:

a) estimate your necessary retirement income in order to maintain your present lifestyle; and

b) identify major sources of retirement income.

A. INTRODUCTION

Many individuals reach retirement and then realize that they should have had a plan because their finances are not adequate. This chapter will enable you to adequately prepare for your retirement. Retirement planning is for everyone. Ideally, retirement planning should begin at least ten to fifteen years prior to retirement. However, the sooner retirement planning begins the better.

B. DETERMINING DESIRED LIFESTYLE

Retirement is that period in our life we anticipate with excitement and enthusiasm. For many it means endless hours fishing or painting pictures or, for some individuals perhaps, a second career working in an area that has always had a particular attraction but might not have afforded an active lifestyle. Whatever is anticipated, we have worked a lifetime to get there. It should be a time of joy.

Retirement is a time to enjoy the fruits of our labour. Yet, only approximately 5% of individuals will be financially sufficient when they reach the age of sixty five (65). In fact, a teenager, eighteen years of age, will likely have more money in his pocket than a man of sixty five has in his bank account. You ask, how can this happen? Well, there are many factors which affect this outcome, none more evident than a lack of financial planning in the earlier years of life.

But we must not lose sight of the fact that it is never too late or too early to plan our financial affairs.

We tend to pass through three major stages in our life cycle. Between the ages of twenty and forty we tend to accumulate assets and during the period of forty to sixty we maintain these things. This is followed by a period of dispersement allowing for self sufficiency until we are called to be with the Lord. We all pass through the first two stages in order to arrive at our retirement. How well we planned our financial affairs in the earlier years will determine how well we will enjoy our retirement years.

1. Why Plan For Retirement?

We need to plan for retirement because most of us are going to reach retirement age. We are living in a country of abundance with great medical facilities and where food and proper care are plentiful. The mortality tables of 1980-82 would indicate that a man aged sixty (60) has a life expectancy of approximately 23 years.

CANADIAN POPULATION PROJECTIONS

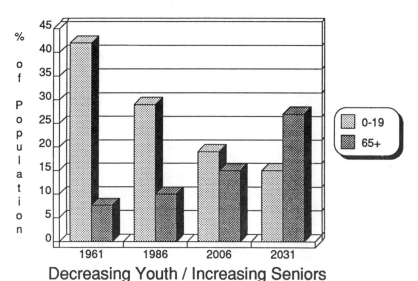

Decreasing Youth / Increasing Seniors

Source: Stats. Can., Cat. 91-520

Fig. 12

A sixty year old of today is likely to be in better physical condition than his/her counterpart of twenty years ago. We see numerous examples of fit, elderly individuals. Roland Mitchner, when Governor General of Canada, could be seen actively exercising around Ottawa. This is a fine example to follow.

We are living in a country where the quality of food and health care services tend to promote long life. There is a change in the balance of ages that is partly due to improved lifestyle conditions and partly do to the falling birth rate. Whereas, in 1961, the ratio of young people to Senior Citizens was approximately 6:1, by the year 2031 this could change to approximately 1:2, if projections are accurate. See Figure 12.

When you retire, there will probably be a decrease in your income which translates into a lifestyle change. Through proper planning, this reduced lifestyle may not occur. In fact, just the opposite is true. Extra funds will allow for extra involvement, giving a more healthy and longer and more active life.

Retirement requires that we make several adjustments. One such adjustment concerns the myth that, when we reach age 65, we should retire. When we receive a pension from our employer, we could consider that pension as a subsidy for income we earn in some other area. Another myth is that we are old. We are older yes, but not old. Old is a state of mind. We still think the way we did at say age twenty one, we just don't move as fast. Our thoughts, of course, are no longer the same, given our maturity[1]

2. Evaluation Of Present Needs

In order for Christians to determine goals and plan their objectives it is necessary to evaluate present requirements. This will mean that we have an opportunity to eliminate unnecessary expenses and to establish new goals and objectives. Using the forms you completed for your short and long term goals in chapter 2, review your new priorities. Secondly, conduct a financial review to determine your present financial picture based on your most recent Asset Evaluation Form, from chapter 2 as well as determining your future needs as indicated from your analysis of Yearly Personal Spending and your Family Budget found in Chapter 4.

3. Evaluation Of Future Needs

Based on your new goals and objectives it is necessary to determine how much money you will need to finance your retirement. You can take your present day financial needs and make a rough estimate using Figure 13. This table allows for inflation and will give you a figure that indicates your expenses in the future if you are to maintain your present day life-style.

For example, let's say you presently require $3,000.00 per month for your financial needs and you plan to retire in the year 2002. Look at the figures in the first three columns. These figures differ according to the rate of inflation. If you estimate a 4% rate, you will need $3,000 X 1.7317, that is, $5,195.10 per month when you reach the year 2002 to maintain the same standard of living (at 4% inflation). Of course, at 5% and 6% inflation rates these figures become $5,939.70 and $6,782.70 per month respectively.

The figure you arrive at for your retirement year may come as a shock, particularly if your projected year is beyond 2000 or if you anticipate a 6% rate of inflation. The message this should convey to you is that there is a need for action now to make some provision for meeting these retirement needs.

We must also recognize that our present monthly/yearly expenses will not necessarily be in effect when we retire. For example, we may still be subjected to taxes, maintenance costs and utility expenses. Our life insurance premiums may not be of the same magnitude though we may still be subject to house and automobile insurance; the latter, perhaps, much increased. On the brighter side, our entertainment, food and medical expenses may consume less of our monies, although these are a function of our general health and lifestyle. Under normal circumstances income taxes will be less upon retirement. Figure 13

4. A More Accurate Estimate

Using your Monthly Fixed and Variable Expenses from chapter 4, examine the figures you have for each item reflecting your current yearly spending. Based on today's figures, consider how these would change, if you had reached retirement now. If, by then, you had paid off all mortgages, and loans on your home, the accommodation figure would change significantly, although there would still be maintenance costs to consider. Other expenses will change similarly. Use the Projected Monthly Retirement Income Form provided to record these new projected expenses. Total the column and divide by twelve. Round the answer to the nearest $100.00. This represents your monthly estimate of expenses if you were to retire now.

We must remember the inflation factor, though. Therefore, do as you did earlier in this chapter. Consult Figure 13 to determine the factor (at 4%, 5%, or 6% inflation) associated with your projected retirement year. Multiply your expected budget by the factor to arrive at an estimated monthly expense in your year of retirement. This should give you the figure that more accurately reflects your needs, as you presently see them, in your retirement year, with the expenses associated with these needs. Naturally, not all contingencies can be accounted for. Major, unexpected changes in certain areas of expense may throw the estimate out but it is the best we can do for now.

We have to set about taking steps to ensure sufficient income for our needs. Let us examine some of the available sources of these monies.

INFLATION ADJUSTMENT TABLE

Instruction: Determine your present monthly budget requirements, combining the information from Monthly Fixed and Variable Expenses and Your Income and Expenditures found in chapter 4. Then locate your year of retirement in the chart below and multiply your total monthly requirement by the factor opposite your year of retirement. (You will notice that the factors change for different projected rates of inflation.) The answer that you arrive at represents the amount of money needed in your year of retirement per month to provide you with the same standard of living you enjoy today at the inflation rate you chose to consider.

Year	4.0%	5.0%	6.0%	7.0%	8.0%	9.0%	10.0%
				Factors			
1988	1.0000	1.0000	1.0000	1.0000	1.0000	1.0000	1.0000
1989	1.0400	1.0500	1.0600	1.0700	1.0800	1.0900	1.1000
1990	1.0816	1.1025	1.1236	1.1449	1.1664	1.1881	1.2100
1991	1.1249	1.1576	1.1910	1.2250	1.2597	1.2950	1.3310
1992	1.1699	1.2155	1.2625	1.3108	1.3605	1.4116	1.4641
1993	1.2167	1.2763	1.3382	1.4026	1.4693	1.5386	1.6105
1994	1.2653	1.3401	1.4185	1.5007	1.5869	1.6771	1.7716
1995	1.3159	1.4071	1.5036	1.6058	1.7138	1.8280	1.9487
1996	1.3686	1.4775	1.5938	1.7182	1.8509	1.9926	2.1436
1997	1.4233	1.5513	1.6895	1.8385	1.9990	2.1719	2.2579
1998	1.4802	1.6289	1.7908	1.9672	2.1589	2.3674	2.5937
1999	1.5395	1.7103	1.8983	2.1049	2.3316	2.5804	2.8531
2000	1.6010	1.7959	2.0122	2.2522	2.5182	2.8127	3.1384
2001	1.6651	1.8856	2.1329	2.4098	2.7196	3.0658	3.4523
2002	1.7317	1.9799	2.2609	2.5785	2.9372	3.3417	3.7975
2003	1.8009	2.0789	2.3966	2.7590	3.1722	3.6425	4.1772
2004	1.8730	2.1829	2.5404	2.9522	3.4259	3.9703	4.5950
2005	1.9479	2.2920	2.6928	3.1588	3.7000	4.3276	5.0545

C. SOURCES OF INCOME IN RETIREMENT

For most people entering retirement, there are four major sources of income. These are:

1. Old Age Security Pension,

2. The Canada Pension, with the additional benefits where applicable,

3. Pension plans provided by former employers; and

4. Personal retirement pension plans and investments.

The amounts involved are standardized from Federal Government sources which are listed in the section below. The private sources of pension or retirement monies through your employer's plan enable you to receive monies in a variety of ways, depending on how the plan was set up. It is advisable, when considering such a plan, to consult with a financial planner for the best way to organize a plan for future benefits.

PROJECTED MONTHLY RETIREMENT INCOME

	Estimated Value	
	Monthly	Yearly
Old Age Security	$ _____	$ _____
Canada Pension	_____	_____
Employer's Pension	_____	_____
Disposable Real Estate	_____	_____
Savings Bonds	_____	_____
R.R.S.P.'s	_____	_____
Life Insurance	_____	_____
Term Deposits	_____	_____
Mutual Funds	_____	_____
Savings Account	_____	_____
Other	_____	_____
Total	$ _____	$ _____

Personal savings and investments may be effected in many ways, from simple savings accounts to tax deferral plans and real estate. These need to be taken into account when planning your budget. The following graph illustrates the potential growth from making annual deposits to your RRSP. The secret is to start early making regular deposits to your savings plan.

RRSP POTENTIAL GROWTH

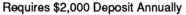

Requires $2,000 Deposit Annually

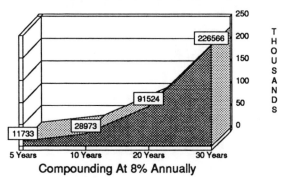

Compounding At 8% Annually

D. SERVICES AVAILABLE TO SENIORS

National

There are a number of benefits and services available to the senior citizen through the offices of the Federal Government. These are listed below with a brief description and directions for obtaining information and assistance.

1. Canada Pension Plan

This plan provides for you and your family against loss of earnings when you retire (as well as if you become disabled or die). The plan is based on annual contributions by you and your employer.

The plan provides for a regular monthly payment upon retirement. This can be at age 65 or earlier, if you wish, which may result in a reduced pension. In either case, it is important to apply at least six months before you turn 65 otherwise you may lose some initial payments.

Also, it is very important that you periodically (every year or two) check that the Record of Earnings, on which your pension will be based, is correct. You should receive a statement as frequent as once a year from the Federal Government. If you have not received a statement, you may do so through the offices indicated below.

Various disability pensions are also available. For married Senior Citizens, there is also provision for benefits on the death of a spouse.

Where To Apply For Canada Pension

Information and application forms for the Canada Pension Plan, which operates throughout Canada, except in Quebec, which has its own plan, may be obtained through the Income Security Programs, Client Service Centers throughout the nation.

Documents Needed When Applying For Canada Pension

When you apply to receive Canada Pension (and likely any other benefit package from the government), you will need to supply the following information (where applicable):

a) Social Insurance Numbers for you and your spouse.

b) Birth and/or baptismal certificates.

c) Marriage certificate.

d) Divorce papers.

e) Address of former spouse.

2. Old Age Security (OAS)

This pension is payable to anyone 65 years of age or over who meets the residence requirements. Again, it is necessary to apply six months prior to reaching age sixty-five.

Where To Apply For OAS

The OAS is administered across Canada through the office of the department of Health and Welfare.

The OAS Identification Card (received automatically) may be used when cashing OAS cheques and to receive discounts and privileges from various merchants across Canada. There are a number of benefits, in addition to the Old Age Security Pension, that you may want to investigate. These include:

> Guaranteed Income Supplement (GIS)
>
> Spouses Allowance
>
> Extended Spouses Allowance
>
> Widowed Spouses Allowance

3. Other

Under certain conditions, you may also want to be aware of the following:

> War Veterans Allowance
> (contact Veterans Affairs Canada)
>
> Veterans Independence Program
> (for veterans with special needs)
>
> Unemployment Insurance Benefit
> (a lump sum payment may be available at age 65. Apply through any Canada Employment Center)

Provincial

Benefits and services offered by each province tend to vary greatly. The list that follows is based on the services found in different Provinces. Not all Provinces are included in this section as some have not responded to our request for information. If you require assistance and your Province has not been mentioned, then read through this material and phone your Provincial offices and ask for departments which offer help as outlined in the following material.

PRINCE EDWARD ISLAND

1. Health

All residents are covered for hospitalization and medical care without premium. The rehabilitation Division of the Department of Health and Social Services supplies prosthetics, wheelchairs and hospital beds at no charge. The unit in Charlottetown provides free physiotherapy. Drugs are provided on a needs basis to those receiving Old Age Security (if not full payment, then at cost price through a provincially operated pharmacy). For further information, call 368-4980 (Charlottetown) or contact one of the regional offices.

2. Accommodation

There are a number of programs to assist homeowners and renters to maintain and adapt their homes. Some Senior Citizens Housing projects, rural and urban, exist with rental fees set according to income. Information may be obtained from the Housing Corporation in Charlottetown.

3. Financial Assistance

Provincial Social Assistance will not supplement the Old Age Security except in special circumstances such as noted above under Health. Other possible sources would include Veterans pensions and Unemployment Insurance.

NOVA SCOTIA

1. Health Insurance Plan

There is a Pharmacare plan for those of 65 years and over who are residents of Nova Scotia and have been registered under the Medical Services Insurance program 429-9700 (Halifax) or (Toll free) 1-429-8880. The Pharmacare card must be applied for when you reach age 65. By using this card Seniors may obtain free prescription drugs.

2. Property Tax Rebate

To qualify, an applicant must be receiving Spouses Allowance or the Guaranteed Income Supplement in January of the year of application and be residing in, and the registered owner of, the home.

3. Rental Assistance

This program provides a monthly rebate to assist Senior Citizens who rent on the private market. An applicant must be receiving the Guaranteed Income Supplement to Old Age Security, Spouses Allowance or have a certain yearly income ceiling and be paying a specified percentage of that income on rent.

4. Senior's Special Assistance

A once a year payment to all Seniors receiving the Guaranteed Income Supplement to Old Age Security is available in March of the year of application. Applications are automatically forwarded to eligible Seniors. For further information on this or other programs indicated above contact the Department of Social Services in Halifax at 424-4500 or any of the regional offices.

5. Housing

The Nova Scotia Department of Housing has a small loans assistance program, a Senior Citizens Public Housing program, a Senior Citizens Assistance program, a Provincial Housing Emergency Repair Program and is involved in the provision of Non-Profit Housing projects. Further information may be obtained from the regional offices. There are also Homes For Special Care for the disabled Senior Citizens who find themselves unable to remain in their own homes even with community support services. For information, call the local municipal services or 424-4277 (Halifax).

QUEBEC

For any information pertaining to the various Health Care Programs provided in Quebec, you must write and request a copy of their book Le Guide des Aines 1987 and include a fee of $9.95. Write To: Ministere des communications Les Publications du Quebec Case postale 1005 Quebec G1K 7B5.

ONTARIO

1. Senior Citizen's Privilege Card

This card can be used for drug benefits under certain circumstances. You should receive this card following your sixty-fifth birthday. For inquiries regarding drug benefits call 965-9451 (Ontario).

2. Gains Benefit

This is related to the Guaranteed Income Supplement and is calculated automatically, if you are receiving GIS. For information call 965-8470 (Ontario).

3. Ontario Health Insurance Plan (OHIP)

Seniors are exempt from paying OHIP premiums. For application information pertaining to exemption at age 65, contact your local OHIP office.

4. Property Tax Grant/Sales Tax Grant

Application forms for these benefits should be received automatically by the recipients of Old Age Security. For additional information, call 965-8470 (Ontario).

5. Financial Assistance

For persons requiring immediate financial aid contact 392-8623 for General Welfare Assistance. For seniors not receiving OAS, women over 60 living alone, seniors supporting dependents, contact 965-1433 (Ontario) for Family Benefits Assistance.

6. Other Benefits And Services

There are many benefits and services provided for Seniors in the area of transportation. Many local and provincial transit systems offer reduced fares for Senior Citizens. In addition, there are special services for disabled Seniors. In Ontario, the following are available:

> Toronto Transit Card for reduced fares.
> Call 392-8701.
> Wheel Trans for the disabled. Call 393-4111.
> Via Rail Services. Call 366-8411.
> Go Transit Services. Call 630-3933.
> Ontario Northland Railway. Call 965-4268.

Information about services for Seniors may also be found in the booklet, "Senior Wise", available free of charge, from the Provincial Government Queens Park, Toronto.

MANITOBA

1. Health Services Commission Plan

All residents are covered by the health insurance plan. For further details regarding registration and coverage, call (collect) 786-7101 (Winnipeg).

2. Social Allowance Health Services

This service provides financial assistance for basic drug, dental and optical supplies and services not covered by the health insurance plan. For eligibility information and assistance, call 944-3744 (Winnipeg) or (Toll free) 1-800-282-8060.

3. Tax Assistance

There are a number of tax assistance programs for Senior Citizens. These include: Manitoba Property Tax Credit, Pensioners School Tax Assistance Credit for Home Owners, Cost of Living Tax Credit. For information, applications and assistance, call 943-3401 (Winnipeg).

4. Supplement For Seniors

This program applies to eligible Seniors who are either 55 to 65 or 65 and over. Application is necessary. Call 945-2686 (Winnipeg) or contact your nearest Community Services office. There are many other plans and programs available to the citizens of Manitoba and information is obtainable from various government departments.

ALBERTA

1. Health Care Insurance Plan

Persons age 65 and older, their spouses and dependents are not required to pay premiums for health insurance. Those already registered with the Plan are sent a Proof of Age questionnaire prior to their 65th birthday. General information regarding registration and cancellation of Health Care or Blue Cross coverage can be found by calling 427-1432 (Edmonton), 297-6411 (Calgary) or any regional office.

2. Financial Aid For Accommodation

There are a number of programs available to assist the citizens of Alberta. For example:

Renters Grant available to those 65 or older who meet the guidelines. Applications are available at Treasury Branches, local city halls or local information centers, or by calling

427-4873 (Edmonton). This also applies to the owners of Mobile Homes and may be applied for on the Renters Grant form.

Property Tax Reduction Benefits up to $1,000 or total taxes is available for those eligible. Application forms are available at your municipal tax office.

Home Heating Protection Program pays a rebate of $100 for each calendar year to eligible seniors. These applications are also available at the local municipal taxation office.

3. Financial Assistance

The Assured Income Plan is related to the Guaranteed Income Supplement and is calculated automatically, if you receive GIS. For information, call 427-7286 (Edmonton).

Social Allowance provides financial help in meeting basic needs. For information, contact the local office of the Alberta Social Services, listed under Government of Alberta in the telephone directory.

The Widow's Pension Program provides financial assistance to widows or widowers, age 55 and over but under 65, who have limited or no income. For information, call 422-4080 (Edmonton).

BRITISH COLUMBIA

1. The Medical Services Plan

An eligible Senior Citizen, prior to turning 65, should receive a Plan A card automatically. This plan provides assistance to permanent residents who are 65 years of age or older. Benefits include reduced dispersing and drug costs. For information, call 387-3724 (Victoria) or Zenith 2179 or 681-9171 (toll-free) from the Lower Mainland.

2. Guaranteed Available Income for Need (GAIN)

GAIN for Senior Citizens is a monthly payment by the provincial government to ensure a guaranteed minimum income level for residents receiving Federal Old Age Security and Guaranteed Income Supplement of Federal Spouse's Allowance. If eligibility exists, it can commence at age 60. No application is necessary. For further information, call 387-4331 (Victoria), 682-0391 (Vancouver) or, toll-free, Zenith 2656.

3. Taxable Income Deductions

The Old Age Exemption and the Pension Income Deduction allow Senior Citizens to deduct from income when calculating taxable income. The Land Tax Deferment Act allows deferment of property taxes on the principal residence until the death of the applicant or transfer of property. For additional information, contact the Ministry of Finance and Corporate Relations.

4. Housing Services

A Home Owner Grant reduces school and municipal taxation for eligible Senior Citizens. Contact the Ministry of Municipal Affairs.

Eligible Senior Citizens may also obtain cash assistance for rental expenses and apply for subsidized and affordable housing (in the Lower Mainland) through the Ministry of Social Services and Housing/B.C. Housing Management Commission (433-1711) in Vancouver.

Local

In most communities across Canada, there are private, non-profit and municipal agencies that will provide information and help to Senior Citizens. In large metropolitan areas, contact the offices for Provincial Government. In Ontario, contact Seniors' Information Service at the offices of the Ministry of Community and Social Services, or obtain the Guide for Senior Citizens Services and Programs in Ontario from the Minister for Senior Citizens' Affairs.

In smaller communities, contact the local municipal offices for information and direction. Frequently, local banks and business organizations honour Senior Citizens through the Old Age Security Identification Card with free or reduced rate banking services and discounted purchases.

E. HEALTH IN RETIREMENT

There is no substitute for a healthy mind, body, and spirit. There is no age limit for these except those which we tend to place upon ourselves. Our thinking process has a strong influence on our attitudes and our abilities. We can be as young as we think or we can be as old as we think.

One of the great pleasures of becoming a Senior Citizen must be the added freedom available to pursue special areas of interest.

Of course, in order to pursue these interests, we must have the funds.

The healthy Senior is one who is active physically, mentally and spiritually. Proper health requires a balance in our lives of exercise, nutritional food, and social involvement. We should consider investing in these areas as well as our finances.

We can invest now for our physical and mental future well-being by adopting a lifestyle that will pay off dividends in the future. This means we must pay attention to our health habits. We should examine our level of physical exercise (does it promote cardiovascular fitness?) and our work/rest ratio (is it balanced?).

We should also consider the area of hobbies; those things we don't really have time for now but when we retire they will provide interesting stimuli.

1. Spiritual Fitness

It is most important to find an active church where you can become involved in worship and social activities. Spiritual fitness is a strong dose of preventive medicine which helps to safeguard against depression and a lack of social contact.

F. SUMMARY

Retirement can be a frightening prospect; so frightening, perhaps, that we are tempted to ignore it, in the hope that it will go away! As we have seen, retirement is something that we must face realistically. We can do this by being aware of our present and future needs and planning accordingly. In this way, we can go a long way toward ensuring that our retirement may be one of rest and enjoyment.

Questions Relating to Retirement

1. Why is retirement planning important for you?
2. List three major sources of retirement income.
3. Explain the relationship between financial health and physical/mental health when planning for retirement.
4. Using the forms provided in this chapter calculate what income you will be earning in your year of retirement. How much income will you have if your pension was 65% of your last year's income?
5. What are the rules regarding your RRSP? Calculate how much money could be deposited into your plan during the next ten years.
6. What are three activities which you could begin, in order to improve or maintain your health in retirement?
7. Contact three persons who have retired during the past ten years. Ask what advice they would give to someone planning to retire the same time as you.

Call your provincial government for details.

Chapter Eight

Handling Financial Freedom

YOUR GOALS

At the close of this chapter, you should be able to:

a) recognize danger signs that suggest you may not be handling your financial freedom wisely.

A. INTRODUCTION

In the chapters above, we have developed plans to overcome various difficulties in our financial management. We should feel good about this. Nevertheless, this last chapter is not intended for self-congratulation. Rather, its purpose is to warn against becoming overconfident, just because we seem to have things under control.

B. THE TRAP

There is also a tendency to feel that we can go it alone, once things begin looking better financially. This applies to everyone, in terms of commitments involving family and counsellors, but, for Christians, in particular, it applies to their relationship with the Lord. He is not there just for us to come to in time of need. Our relationship should be a constant one that recognizes His supremacy in our lives, regardless of our circumstances.

When we are accustomed to debt, and struggling to make ends meet, we are living in a future-oriented society based on deficit financing. When we find that we no longer have any debt, we tend to think we are rich, sometimes resulting in our spending our way back into debt.

Remember that we desire to maintain a positive cash flow at all times. For this reason we should not carry credit cards or cheques which make it easy for us to walk back into debt. The obvious solution is to pay cash. When we pay for our purchases with cash, it is a strong dose of reality that reminds us of how difficult it is to earn money and how easy it is to spend.

C. EARLY WARNING SIGNS

One of the very early warning signs is a return to using credit cards. Many times, because we have a zero balance in our credit card account, we feel that we can resume using our cards because we have the situation under control. Another sign is using credit to make a purchase with the intent to pay off the credit balance when we get our next pay check. This is, in effect, borrowing against future earnings. The question that must be asked is: is the article so important that you must have it now, even if you have to make credit payments for it?

Suddenly, you can afford items more expensive than those you have been purchasing in the past. There is a temptation to adopt a more expensive lifestyle. This may make you feel good. It may be that you want to reward yourself for getting out of debt. It is also a good way to get back into that debt and it certainly will prevent you from making investments for your future well-being.

There is also a tendency to feel that we can go it alone, once things begin looking better financially. This applies to everyone, in terms of commitments involving family and counsellors, but, for Christians, in particular, it applies to their relationship with the Lord. He is not there just for us to come to in time of need. Our relationship should be a constant one that recognises His supremacy in our lives, regardless of our circumstances.

While He does not change[1], worldly things do, including tax regulations and various other financially related procedures that influence our lives. Consequently, we cannot afford to ignore changing events as they apply to our financial planning. A financial plan is not carved in stone. It must be subject to review as circumstances change and we must be prepared to carry out periodic reviews with our advisers.

D. HELPING OTHERS TO FINANCIAL FREEDOM

One of our goals is to teach Christians stewardship principles and the management of God's resources based on His principles. The success of our program is based upon your commitment to achieving financial freedom. As well, we desire to see our graduates teaching others about His principles, so that they may also be good stewards and live debt free for Him.

You are now in a position where you can set an example for others by telling them how you got out from under the debt load and by demonstrating good stewardship of those resources loaned to you by our Lord.

E. SUMMARY

We are committed and devoted to helping as many individuals as possible. If, after the course contained in this book is completed, and you find that you still require assistance, then please contact us for help. You may reach us by completing the post card at the back of this book.

Glossary

FINANCIAL TERMS

Administrator	This is a person appointed by a court to administer and settle the estate of someone dying without a Will.
Amortization Schedule	A financial table which illustrates a mortgage repayment by presenting the opening balance, the interest paid and the closing balance.
Annuity	A series of equal payments made to an individual on an annual basis.
Assets	Anything owned by an individual or a corporation.
Balance Sheet	A financial statement which shows the net worth, assets and liabilities of an individual or corporation at a particular point in time.
Blended Payments	The repayment of a debt in equal payments of principal and interest, on a regular basis for a specific period of time.
Budget	A financial document which contains revenues and expenses over a period of time. It is necessary in any financial plan.
Cash Flow	Cash flow is the amount of cash available from your pay cheque after deductions. It specifically refers to the cash coming in and the cash paid out during a period of time.
Cash Surrender Value	The amount of cash received if a particular type of life insurance policy was terminated.

Compound Interest	This is the amount of interest, earned or paid, on interest previously earned.
Current Asset	A current asset is easily converted into cash.
Debt	An obligation to pay an amount to someone or some corporation in the future.
Defined Benefit Plan	This is a pension which provides a certain level of pension, expressed as either a certain dollar amount or as a percentage of pensionable earnings for each year of service under the plan.
Dividend Tax Credit	This is a tax credit allowed against income earned through investing in Canadian companies. As a result, income earned through dividends is taxed at a lower rate.
Equity	Equity is the difference between your assets and your liabilities. Sometimes called Net Worth.
Estate Planning	A process of planning for the maximum dispersement of assets, incurring minimum taxation and shrinkage following one's death.
Executor	A person (male) appointed in a Will to settle the financial affairs and other obligations of the deceased.
Executrix	A person (female) appointed in a Will to settle the financial affairs and other obligations of the deceased.
Financial Plan	A process of evaluating present financial status with a view to achieving future financial requirements.
Fixed Assets	Assets which are not easily converted into cash such as buildings, land etc.
Fixed Expenses	These are expenses which occur on a regular basis and do not vary in the amount.
Goals	The task which you are trying to accomplish through implementing various financial objectives.

Gross Income	The amount of income earned before any deductions.
Guaranteed Income Certificates	A certificate issued by a financial institution with a guarantee to pay a predetermined rate of interest for a stipulated period of time.
Guaranteed Income Supplement	An amount of money paid to retired person with limited income and is not subject to taxation.
Guardian	An individual appointed in a Will to provide on-going care for a minor or individual(s) with "special" needs.
Impulse Buying	Making a purchase without giving prior thought to the particular purchase.
Income Splitting	The process of dividing income among family members so as to pay less tax.
Inflation	The amount of increase in the cost of living, or the decrease in your purchasing power, usually measured in percentage terms.
Intestate	This term refers to someone who dies without leaving a Will.
Liabilities	Any money owed to an individual or a corporation. A summary of the amounts owing appear on the Balance Sheet.
Long Term Goals	Usually referring to goals which will take longer than one year to obtain.
Long Term Objectives	Usually objectives which will run longer than one year and are directed toward achieving long term goals.
Money Purchase	A plan which provides a pension based on whatever pension income can be purchased at retirement from accumulated contributions and investment earnings in the plan.
Mutual Fund	An investment company which combines the money of many people whose investment goals are similar. The funds are usually invested in a wide variety of securities to provide stability and safety in the event of large price changes in a particular security.

Net Income	The income remaining after deductions from total income have been taken and before deductions for personal exemptions have been taken.
Objectives	The tasks that must be accomplished in order to reach a particular goal.
Positive Cash Flow	Having more money flowing in each period than what is flowing out each period.
RESP	A Registered Education Savings Plan is an income-splitting plan designed to lower taxes of parents or grandparents. There is no tax deduction for contributions but income earned on the contribution accumulates tax free inside the plan.
Retirement Planning	The process of planning for financial security in the retirement years. Ideally, this planning process begins at least ten to twenty years before retirement.
RRSP	Registered Retirement Saving Plan is the name given to a voluntary payment to a private pension by an individual. It is a tax deferral plan which allows money in the plan to compound tax free until the funds are withdrawn. This plan ends at age 71.
RPP	This is an employer-sponsored pension plan and may be either a defined benefit or money purchase type.
Short Term Objectives	These are tasks which aid one in achieving their goals and are usually accomplished in less than one year.
Short Term Goals	Usually referring to goals which will be accomplished in less than one year.
Tax Credit	The amount of money deducted directly from the tax owing.
Tax Shelter	The creation of a tax loss to offset an individual's taxable income and in doing so reduce the amountof current tax payable.

Taxable Income	The amount of income after all deductions and credits have been applied. This the amount on which tax owing is calculated.
Term Deposits	An amount of money held on deposit with a financial institution for a specific period of time at a fixed rate of return.
Testamentary Trust	This is at trust which becomes effective as the result of a Will.
Tithe	A tithe is one-tenth. A biblical term used in the Bible to offer a guideline for giving.
Variable Expenses	Expenses which are subject to change as a result of certain circumstances which may be beyond your control.
Year-End Tax Plan	The process of analyzing your tax situation for the current year and determining necessary action to lower taxes.

Appendix

YOUR PERSONAL EVALUATION QUESTIONNAIRE

	YES	NO
1. Do you have a written financial plan?	☐	☐
2. Have you and your spouse prepared your "Will"?	☐	☐
3. Do you know the amount of your family debt?	☐	☐
4. Do you have money left over at the end of the month?	☐	☐
5. Have you started an R.R.S.P.?	☐	☐
6. Do you have a plan to pay off your mortgage early?	☐	☐
7. Do you have a plan for making future investments?	☐	☐
8. Do you worry about paying bills and meeting financial obligations?	☐	☐
9. Do you pay all of your bills on time?	☐	☐
10. Have you had to borrow money to pay off debts or taxes?	☐	☐
11. Do you hold a second job in order to meet your financial obligations?	☐	☐
12. Are you presently "tithing" your income on a regular basis?	☐	☐
13. Do you have more than one automobile?	☐	☐
14. Do you plan your shopping to avoid impulse buying?	☐	☐
15. Do you discuss major purchases with your spouse before a purchase?	☐	☐
16. Do you always receive a tax receipt for your charitable giving?	☐	☐
17. Do you use personal credit cards?	☐	☐
18. Do you know the balance of your bank accounts?	☐	☐

Source: T. Giordano, CBN, Virginia Beach

Name: _____

SUMMARY ASSET EVALUATION FORM

ASSETS		LIABILITIES	
Chequing Accounts	$ _____	Bank Loans	$ _____
Savings Accounts	_____	Charge Accounts	_____
Life Ins. Cash Value	_____	Monthly Bills O/S	_____
Money Owed You	_____	Other	_____
Gold/Silver	_____		
Securities/Stocks	_____	Mortgage/Home	_____
CSB's	_____	Cottage	_____
Mutual Funds	_____	Other	_____
GIC's	_____		
Business	_____	Debts/Individuals	_____
Other	_____	Credit Union	_____
Personal Property		**Loans**	
Automobiles	_____	Automobiles	_____
House Furnishings	_____	Rec. Vehicles	_____
Antiques/Jewelery	_____	Other	_____
Real Estate			
Home	_____	**TOTAL LIABILITY** $ _____	
Cottage	_____		
Condo	_____		
Other	_____		
Pension		**NET WORTH**	
Company	_____		
RRSP's	_____	Total Assets	$ _____
Annuities	_____	Less	
Insurance Face Value	_____	Total Liabilities	$ _____
Insurance FV Spouse	_____		
Other	_____	Net Estate	$ _____
TOTAL ASSETS	$ _____	Dated _____	

Name: _____

SHORT TERM GOALS

Prioritized Goals   **Prioritized Goals**

1.   1.

2.   2.

3.   3.

COMBINED SHORT TERM GOALS

1.

2.

3.

Name: _____

LONG TERM GOALS

Prioritized Goals   **Prioritized Goals**

1.   1.

2.   2.

3.   3.

COMBINED LONG TERM GOALS

1.

2.

3.

ESTABLISHING OBJECTIVES
For Goal # _____

Prioritized Objectives   **Prioritized Objectives**

1.   1.

2.   2.

3.   3.

COMBINED OBJECTIVES

1.

2.

3.

PERSONAL TIME CHART

Name: _____ Date: _____

	J F M A M J J A S O N D
1. Goal:	
Objective 1.	
Objective 2.	
Objective 3.	
2. Goal:	
Objective 1.	
Objective 2.	
Objective 3.	
3. Goal:	
Objective 1.	
Objective 2.	
Objective 3.	

ANALYSIS OF YEARLY PERSONAL SPENDING

	Paid Out Last Year	Reduce Next Year
Cash Withdrawals	$ _____	$ _____
Charitable Giving	_____	_____
Rent/Mortgage	_____	_____
Food	_____	_____
Entertainment (Restaurants, Events, Etc.)	_____	_____
Credit Card Payments	_____	_____
Bank Loans	_____	_____
Clothing Items	_____	_____
Medical	_____	_____
Utilities	_____	_____
Telephone	_____	_____
Vacations	_____	_____
Personal Allowances	_____	_____
Savings	_____	_____
Transportation (Public, Car, Gasoline, Maintenance, Etc.)	_____	_____
Home Improvements	_____	_____
Unspecified Cash	_____	_____
Miscellaneous	_____	_____
TOTALS	$ _____	$ _____

1. Did you receive lasting value for money paid out?
2. Did you indicate where you could reduce spending next year?

SOURCES OF MONTHLY INCOME

	Amount
Present employment	$ _____
Spousal employment	_____
Part-time employment	_____
Investments	_____
Interest on money invested	_____
Money owed you/paid monthly	_____
Other	_____
TOTAL MONTHLY INCOME	$ _____

MONTHLY INCOME AND EXPENDITURES

Total Income	$ _____
Deduct: Total Expenditures	$ _____
NET BALANCES	$ _____

MONTHLY FIXED EXPENSES

	Amount
Tithe	$ _____
Rent/Mortgage	_____
Insurance	_____
Bank Loans	_____
Health Insurance	_____
Saving Program	_____
TOTAL MONTHLY FIXED EXPENSES	$ _____

MONTHLY VARIABLE EXPENSES

	Amount
Food (At Home, Restaurants)	$ _____
Transportation (Ins., Gas, Fares	_____
Clothing	_____
Recreation	_____
Vacations	_____
Utilities (Heat, Hydro, Water)	_____
Home Improvements	_____
Other	_____
TOTAL MONTHLY VARIABLE EXPENSES	$ _____

THE FAMILY BUDGET

INCOME		Monthly
Present Employment	$	_____
Spousal Employment		_____
Part-Time Employment		_____
Investment Interest		_____
Canada Pension		_____
Old Age Security		_____
Private Pension		_____
Other		_____
TOTAL INCOME	$	_____
EXPENSES		
Food	$	_____
Shelter		_____
Transportation		_____
Entertainment		_____
Recreation		_____
Security		_____
Charitable Donations		_____
Utilities		_____
Taxes		_____
Debt Payment		_____
Investments		_____
Medical Expenses		_____
Clothing		_____
Personal		_____
Other		_____
TOTAL EXPENSES	$	_____

Notes
Chapter 1

1. 2 Co. 1:22
2. Jos. 1:6; Dt. 1:21
3. Lk. 16:1,2; Mt. 6:20,21
4. Mt. 25:31-36
5. Mt. 6:33; Ps. 37:4
6. 1 Pe. 5:7
7. Jn. 10:10; 3:15,16; Ps. 65:11
8. Ps. 34:4
9. Ro. 6:23; Pr. 16:10; Ro. 1:32
10. Php. 4:19
11. Mt. 10:30
12. Mal. 3:11
13. Nu. 23:19
14. Pr. 3:5,6; Ps. 4:5; Isa. 26:4; Ps. 37:4-6

Chapter 2

1. Mt. 25:14-30; Lk. 16:1-13
2. Hag. 2:8; Ps. 24:1; 89:11
3. Php. 4:19
4. Gal. 3:13,14,29
5. Gal. 6:7; 1Co. 4:2; Lk. 6:38
6. Pr. 16:3; 3:5,6
7. Pr. 15:22
8. Pr. 3:13; 14:8; 24:3,4
9. Lk. 14:28-31
10. Pr. 16:9; 26:12; Isa. 1:19; Mt. 6:33
11. Jas. 4:13,14; Pr. 27:1; Lk. 12:18-20; Ps. 39:5; 102:3
12. Php. 3:14; 1Co. 9:24
13. Gal. 6:9; Jas. 1:12; 1Co. 15:58; Heb. 12:3; Rev. 2:10
14. Dt. 28:1-14; 3Jn. 2:2; Php. 4:19; Lk. 6:38; Mk. 10:29,30
15. Mt. 18:18; Jn. 15:7; 1Jn 5:14,15
16. 1Co. 3:6-9; 2Co. 9:6
17. Jas. 1:6-8; Pr. 16:3; 3:5,6
18. Mt. 6:33; Jn. 15:7; Ps. 37:4; 21:2

Chapter 3

1. Dt. 28:12,13; 15:8
2. Pr. 11:25; 28:27; 28:8; Ne. 57-11; Eze. 18:13
3. Ge. 1:26-28; 3:8,9
4. Dt. 28:1-14; 29:9; 30:15,16
5. Jn. 10:10
6. Jn. 10:10; 3Jn. 2:2
7. Mt. 6:33; Jos. 1:7-9; Mk. 10:29,30
8. 1Ti. 4:8; 1Jn. 5:11-13
9. La. 3:40; Ps. 119:59; 139:23,24
10. Jn. 17:14
11. Php. 4:12
12. Jas. 4:7

13. Ps. 94:12; 1Co. 11:32; Dt. 8:38; Heb. 12:5,6
14. 2Ki. 4:7; Lk. 12:32-34; Ro. 13:8
15. Mt. 22:21; Le. 27:31
16. 1Co. 15:58

Chapter 4

1. Pr. 2:6
2. Pr. 1:7
3. Pr. 3:5; 3:13; Ps. 32:8, 37:4,5; 16:3
4. Dt. 7:9; 1Co. 1:9; Heb. 10:23
5. Ps. 34:4
6. Col. 1:9
7. Pr. 19:20
8. Ps. 33:11
9. Ps. 1:1
10. Ps. 37:4, 5; 32:8; Pr. 16:3; Jas. 1:5; Eph. 5:17
11. Pr. 12:15; 15:22; 1Co. 12:8
12. Lk. 14:28-30; Pr. 24:3,4
13. 1Co. 9:24-27

Chapter 5

1. Ps. 42:1; 50:10; Hag. 2:8
2. Ge. 1:1
3. Lev. 25:23
4. Pr. 3:9
5. Mt. 25:14-30
6. 1Ti. 5:8
7. Gal. 6:9
8. Mk. 12:17
9. Mt. 25:23
10. 1Ti. 5:8
11. Lk. 1:37
12. Eph. 3:20
13. 1 Co. 3:6,7
14. Mt. 25:29
15. Mt. 6:33
16. Ge. 15:7; Jos 1:11

Chapter 6

1. Rom. 13:7; Mt. 22:21
2. Mat. 10:10b; 1Ti. 5:18

Chapter 7

1. 1Co. 13:11

Chapter 8

1. Num. 23:19; Mal. 3:6; Jas.1:17

Notes

Notes

Notes

YES!

I'm interested in a personal financial planning consultant coming to visit me at my convenience.

☐ In my home   ☐ In my office

Date Preferred _____   Time Preferred _____ AM / PM

Name: _____

Address: _____

City: _____ Prov: _____ Postal Code: _____

Phone: Home ( ) _____ Office ( ) _____

Birthdate: _____ Spouse's Birthdate _____

Areas of interest:

☐ Will Preparation/Review   ☐ Tax Planning
☐ Retirement Planning   ☐ Budgeting
☐ Seminar In My Area   ☐ Financial Planning
                                     ☐ Newsletter

Business Reply Mail
No postage necessary
if mailed in Canada.

Postage will be paid by

Att: Financial Planning Dept.

CROSSROADS CHRISTIAN COMMUNICATIONS INC.
100 Huntley Street
Toronto, Ontario
M4Y 9Z9

Canada Post
Postes Canada
27094